'A stimulating and vital book that
giving both as "obligation" an⟨
blessing others and being blesse⟨
Rev Canon J John

'Wendy has written a winner! Books on giving and being
generous usually fall into one of two categories: Shame on you
for not giving or Here's how to do it because it worked for me.
This book is neither of these. Here stories of generosity are
historical, accurate, simple, varied and inspirational. The
challenge that Wendy presents is really an opportunity to catch
the heartbeat of Father God who so loved the world that He
gave. If you are a giver, you will be inspired to keep on giving.
If you haven't yet discovered the joy of being generous, this is
the book for you to start that journey.'
*Steve Long, Former Senior Leader of Catch the Fire Church (Toronto);
author*

'Having known Wendy since we started theological college
together, it is a joy to see the fruit of her years of experience in
the financial sector and Christian ministry come together in
print in this book. Wendy has a gift of drawing together godly
practical wisdom with theological insight in her own inimitable
style, which is simultaneously straight-talking, humorous and
accessible. The questions at the end of each chapter are really
useful to ponder, and help ensure this book is one that not only
informs our thinking, but also should inspire us into action.'
*Jenny Kimble, Dean of Undergraduate Studies, Regents Theological
College, UK*

'Wendy has drawn together a blueprint, a guide and a rallying
cry for followers of Christ to imagine a world where giving is
normal, generosity is our standard and we give to every good
cause on every occasion.'
*Don Esson, Director of Partnerships and Development, Spurgeons and
Founder, Prime Leadership Solutions*

'This is a book that makes you think again about generous giving. You are not left condemned, but inspired. Wendy very skilfully, with humility and humour, navigates a subject many shy away from. The reader, whatever their gifting or financial position, is sensitively encouraged to step out into the exciting arena and the blessing of generous giving.'
Richard Giles, Chair of Sat 7

'Challenging, inspiring and practical. This book will profoundly impact the generosity of those who read it and there will be a far-reaching impact for the gospel as a result.'
Gavin Calver, CEO of Evangelical Alliance

'This little book has a big message for followers of Jesus, encouraging us to be joyful, generous and radical givers. Full of practical ideas, true stories and challenging questions, Wendy's cheerful style inspires us to a generosity that will outlast our lifetime. It's well worth the read.'
Ruth Walker, mentoring and strategy specialist; non-executive director, charity board member and chair

'Spending any time at all in Wendy's company is to be cajoled, cheered up, jollied, encouraged and challenged all at once. You come away reminded of why it's both essential AND great to be a follower of Jesus! She has a knack of linking you back to the core of what's important about life and faith, with oodles of joy and fun. This book feels like Wendy has stood up, tapped her glass, gained everyone's attention and then announced that we all need to look with fresh eyes at a subject that British Christianity doesn't normally touch with a bargepole: financial generosity. Filled with sound biblical wisdom, solid research, inspirational stories, interesting anecdotes and more than a few truly crazy testimonies of God's power and generosity, Wendy has written something that will really inspire us all to reconsider how we think about our finances in a much more godly way.'
Rev Nick and Chloe Whittome, Birmingham City Church

Generous with a Capital G

Wendy Pawsey

instant
apostle

First published in Great Britain in 2024

Instant Apostle
104A The Drive
Rickmansworth
Herts
WD3 4DU

British Library Cataloguing-in-Publication Data

A catalogue record for this book is available from the British Library.

This book and all other Instant Apostle books are available from Instant Apostle:

Website: www.instantapostle.com

Email: info@instantapostle.com

ISBN 978-1-912726-83-7

Printed in Great Britain.

Dedication

I dedicate this labour of love to my husband, Marcus, who has always been my biggest cheerleader, encouraged me when the doubts have set in and respected my need to occasionally wallow like a hippo.

Contents

Foreword

In my personal experience, being the receiver of a financial or practical gift, given selflessly with love and no strings attached, is both a humbling and a gratitude-inducing thing. It has expanded my view of God as the giver of all good things, and my heartfelt gratitude to a generous donor in the past has later translated into a deep thankfulness also to God. Entering into my adult years I decided I would set about becoming, wherever possible, a generous giver. Just as so many people had blessed me in all manner of practical, financial or supportive ways – helping to fund ministry projects I was a part of – I decided that I too wanted to be part of making people feel genuinely valued, supported, cheered on and celebrated.

Against the current backdrop of a deeply challenging cultural landscape and significant practical, emotional and financial need among so many in our wider communities, what better time is there for us, as practising Christians and the UK Church, to adopt and grow into a posture of generous and abundant giving, along with compassion and a love for others which can result in a great many lives transformed by a recognition of God's love in action?

This timely book, written by my wonderfully gifted and inspiring friend and colleague, Rev Wendy Pawsey, speaks to us about the power and potential impact of generous giving. It challenges the reader to lean in and heed the nudge of the Holy Spirit, and to act on it in a way that not only provides for those in need and in God's service, but in doing so also brings glory to God. As Head of Mission for the Evangelical Alliance, I desire to see people, across the length and breadth of the UK, both inside and outside our churches, encounter something so powerful of the love of Jesus that makes them ask questions, sense God's care and provision for them and come into a life-giving relationship with Him. Maybe encouraging a culture of generous and sacrificial giving in many of our churches is a good place to begin.

Based on her fascinating survey results and on references rooted in both historical stories and biblical truths, Wendy brings great wisdom, insight and challenge – prompting us all to catch the spirit of generosity which is so needed in our culture. She unpacks for the reader what we can learn from Jesus' teachings, His encounters with others and the multiplication of the blessings on individuals or crowds when He was obedient to His Father God. Wendy, with great humour, personal stories, learned experience and reference to our mandate as Christian witnesses, implores readers of all ages to adopt a posture of Christlike giving. She outlines with energy and encouragement that such giving can be both revolutionary and a game-changer to those on the receiving end – opening doors to greater relationships and life-giving conversations that speak of Jesus' proximity and goodness to them as a cared-for individual, leaving the reader with the poignant question to consider: 'Is generosity the new evangelism?'

I can wholeheartedly recommend this book for leaders as inspiring content to fuel a sermon series, for individuals or for small groups to read, engage, discuss and interact with. The reflection questions at the end of each chapter are a brilliant tool for igniting a conversation or self-reflection around kindness, generosity, friendships and our relationship with money – all of which provoke encouragement and challenge around our own or corporate practices of giving, tithing and beyond. Wendy also encourages leaders in developing strategic vision – considering and praying for financial provision and fundraising opportunities, recognising that giving, too, forms part of our worship to God.

In a world where it is often countercultural to give abundantly, generously and selflessly, may you be encouraged by this book, strengthened and equipped by the Holy Spirit, and may you take great delight in becoming a generous giver. May you know too God's provision in your own life, and that by blessing others you will see many friends, peers, colleagues or neighbours drawn closer to Jesus as a direct result of your actions and generosity. What a privilege, responsibility and joy. My gratitude to Wendy for writing this book, to prompt us on this journey and further equip us as to how best we can, powerfully and together, make Jesus known to those He has put around us. We pray to see many, many lives impacted by the gospel as a direct result of our obedience and giving in the years to come.

Rachael Heffer, Head of Mission, Evangelical Alliance

Introduction

For many years I'd stumble across articles about tithing, gifts and offerings and would skim-read with a vague promise to myself that I'd properly study this topic later. Then seemingly more pressing subjects such as evangelism, cultural decline and my growing ironing pile ensured this date was a long time in coming... or maybe God was waiting for the perfect moment.

In 2016, after much prayer, I moved away from being a full-time minister and embraced being bi-vocational. Instead of returning to the world of finance, in which I was well versed, I dived into the crazy world that is fundraising. In this new environment I found myself surrounded by a multitude of amazing people who gave generously and lavishly to causes that were close to their hearts.

Seeing generosity of this scale on an almost daily basis made me curious. I understood tithing, I regularly gave gifts and would respond to offerings. My time in church had exposed me to some seriously generous giving that on more than one occasion involved cars and foreign holidays.

But the level of giving I was witnessing within the fundraising world was off the scale, was generous with a neon flashing capital G, and my mind was blown with the difference that could be made for His kingdom if more people practised financial generosity. The world we live in could be dramatically enhanced; Christian organisations, churches, outreaches and missions would be able to reach more people with the gospel and be properly resourced. More and more people would have access to the good news, hope and love that is Jesus. Exciting stuff!

After much study, many conversations, gentle encouragement and some serious prompting from God, I have tried to compile in this book some of what I have learned and witnessed, with the aim of encouraging you to change the world by expanding your generosity. This has been an incredibly enjoyable process and I am so grateful to the Holy Spirit for His constant inspiration. I could not have written this alone!

I'm aware there are many ways that generosity can be expressed, such as time, encouragement and emotional availability, to name a few, but the focus of this book is on financial generosity. This isn't because I believe it to be the most important area of generosity, but simply because this is the area where I feel God has equipped me to share. I've never been afraid to address tough subjects, and money is arguably one of the most confusing and sensitive issues for Christians.

With this in mind, to reduce the level of bias and enable me to share a broader view than my own, I asked a wide range of lovely people from different denominations and demographics to complete a survey focusing on financial generosity. The survey is a mix of open-ended and closed questions exploring different aspects, opinions and experiences. The results of this will pop up in the relevant spaces, will always be referred to simply as 'the survey' and is available for you to read in its entirety towards the end of the book. As it contains the thoughts, feelings and experiences of fifty Christians, it makes for interesting reading. Some of the responses have been lightly edited for this book.

There are ten chapters in this book, with each chapter finishing with some questions to ponder – the idea being that you spend a few minutes delving deeper into the contents of that particular topic and consider what you believe, why you believe it and if the Holy Spirit is prompting you to act.

If you are reading this book as part of a small group, be enriched by others. If you are reading by yourself, make some notes on the stories and scriptures that jump out at you, and chat them through with a trusted Christian friend. At every step of the way, ask the Holy Spirit to bring greater enlightenment.

My heartfelt prayer is that you enjoy this book, that on occasion it will make you smile, at times it may make you frown, but ultimately you will wholeheartedly embrace a life of crazy generosity and be guided and challenged to become more like Jesus. To help you achieve this I have included 'The Thiry-day Generosity Challenge', with the idea being that you have fun and renew your mind by living out some of what you have read. As a preacher, I always try to include something for the head, heart and hands within my sermons: the contents of the book will address your head and heart; the challenge is for your hands.

Before you begin, I want to provide one last motivation. Those who embrace or feel called to a generous life will be people who leave a legacy. Generosity doesn't exist in a vacuum and is not just about the giver or the recipient. A generous life touched by God has the power to exceed our lifetime. Irrespective of whether we are just beginning our time on earth or are closer to being promoted to glory, what we do today shapes the legacy we leave tomorrow. The good news is every single person, without exception, has the potential to create a legacy of generosity.

To kick-start us on this journey, John Rinehart from Gospel Patrons has kindly allowed me to share this poem… enjoy!

The Gospel Patrons Recipe
In every generation, God looks for people to use.
The question we must ask is what kind our Lord will
    choose.
Is it the bold, the strong, the wealthy, the wise?
The best in class or beautiful to the eyes?
No, my friends, that is not where our God starts.
For man looks on the outside, but God looks at the
    heart.

Men and women who would see a generation won,
Are those who learn to say, 'Not my will, but yours be
    done.'
Like Job, they know the God who gives and takes
    away.
Like James and John, they drop their nets when they
    hear their Master say:
'Come, follow me, my friends, and redirect your life.
From now on you'll be catching men, and freeing
    them from strife.'

'Here am I! Send me,' was Isaiah's reply.
'I too will go,' Esther said, 'whether I live or I die.'
The ones who enlist and answer God's call,
Are the people prepared to lay down their all.
A willing investment, a life freely laid down,
Is the seed of a movement, the cross before the crown.

Don't go it alone, is the second core piece.
This is no solo journey when seeking lost sheep.
Partners we are in the work of the Lord,
One going, one giving, but both fully on board.
One speaking, one sending, we'll both play our part,
Charging ahead as lights in the dark.

Joanna for Jesus and Phoebe for Paul,
Friends for the road whether it rises or falls.
Call Gaius and Barnabas up to the mic,
Hear their stories of power when God's lightning did
    strike.
They were selflessly seeking the glory of God,
True partners together and best as a squad.

The end is ahead and it's always been the same,
King Jesus enthroned with a name above names.
And a multitude around him from every tribe, nation
    and tongue,
Declaring his praises as the ones who've been sprung
From death, from the grave, from hell, and from sin.
The saints in their glory are his prize, we're his win.

There's a message, there's news, which will lead to
    this day.
It's the story of him who was the truth, life and way.

Our salvation, our hope, our all rests in him,
Who's the Alpha, Omega, Beginning and End.

So 'Preach Jesus, preach Jesus, preach Jesus,' we cry.
And we'll stand by your side till our faith becomes sight.
Play your part, run your race, fight your fight to the end.
We are gospel proclaimers and gospel patrons.[1]

Amen!

---

[1] www.gospelpatrons.org/articles/the-gospel-patrons-recipe (accessed 28th April 2023).

1
We're Going on a Bear Hunt[2]

For several years I helped out in various groups that my children attended or family members ran, and one thing they all had in common was the use of the chant-aloud book that focused on a family going on a bear hunt.

At the time we didn't consider how the bear would feel about being hunted, but as instructed we did pat our legs, wave our arms, grip the side of our face and respond to the sense of drama as the leader explained there was no avoiding the long grass in pursuit of the bear, and we would need to walk through the grass.

And before we look at anything else, I want us to walk through and examine the meaning of generosity. Generous giving takes us to a whole new realm where we give extravagantly of our time, talent and treasure. This is the adoption, the fostering of a lifestyle where we freely give to others out of our abundance.

The clever folks at The University of Notre Dame, Indiana, USA, tell us that the modern English word 'generosity' finds its origins in the Latin word *generōsus*,

---

[2] *We're Going on a Bear Hunt* is a British chant-aloud children's book written by Michael Rosen (London: Walker Books, 1993).

which means 'of noble birth'. During the seventeenth century this changed, and generosity moved away from being applied to those of noble birth and was aligned more closely to a nobility of spirit. This continued to evolve, and during the eighteenth century the understanding of generosity was affiliated with the giving away of money and possessions. Rather concerning is the conclusion that today's understanding of the word still carries remnants of its historical meaning and leaves some feeling excused from practising generosity because of their 'more ordinary perceived status'.[3]

Thankfully this is not what we see in Scripture.

One of my favourite passages is Matthew 25:34-40:

> Then the King will say to those on his right, 'Come, you who are blessed by my Father; take your inheritance, the kingdom prepared for you since the creation of the world. For I was hungry and you gave me something to eat, I was thirsty and you gave me something to drink, I was a stranger and you invited me in, I needed clothes and you clothed me, I was ill and you looked after me, I was in prison and you came to visit me.'
>
> Then the righteous will answer him, 'Lord, when did we see you hungry and feed you, or thirsty and give you something to drink? When did we see you a stranger and invite you in, or needing clothes and clothe you? When did we see you ill or in prison and go to visit you?'

---

[3] www.generosityresearch.nd.edu/more-about-the-initiative/what-is-generosity (accessed 6th June 2023).

> The King will reply, 'Truly I tell you, whatever you did for one of the least of these brothers and sisters of mine, you did for me.'

As a more literal translation from the Greek of 'you who are blessed by my Father' is actually 'blessed ones who belong to my Father', the only barrier I see to generosity being practised, if you are a Christian, is faith and belief.[4] As we proceed through this book, you will read many inspiring and obtainable examples of others' faith and belief.

The financial generosity survey that accompanies this book contained the question, 'On a scale of 1-10 (1 being low, 10 being high), how generous would you rate yourself?' That's a tough question! However, the average score was 7.32, which is above midway and, if I'm being honest, higher than I'd guessed it would be. But I wonder what it would take to move that score up to 8.32, 9.32 or even a full-on 10? What needs to happen to close the gap and be someone who actively seeks opportunities to be abundantly generous?

As Christians have a history of generosity, could it be higher?

To answer this question, bear with me as I attempt to take you back in time. To set the scene, we need to remember that the whole Bible bears witness to the generous nature of God, so let's start with Scripture.

Psalm 145:8-9 declares:

---

[4] www.biblehub.com/commentaries/ellicott/matthew/25.htm (accessed 21st June 2023).

> The LORD is gracious and compassionate,
> slow to anger and rich in love.
> The LORD is good to all;
> he has compassion on all he has made.

While Proverbs 14:31 proclaims:

> Whoever oppresses the poor shows contempt for
> their Maker,
> but whoever is kind to the needy honours God.

That is our God! Later on, in James 2:14-17 we are informed:

> What good is it, my brothers and sisters, if someone claims to have faith but has no deeds? Can such faith save them? Suppose a brother or a sister is without clothes and daily food. If one of you says to them, 'Go in peace; keep warm and well fed,' but does nothing about their physical needs, what good is it? In the same way, faith by itself, if it is not accompanied by action, is dead.

Such strong words and an unmistakable call to act generously – 'faith by itself, if it is not accompanied by action, is dead'. Take a moment to think about that, to really let the words – and more importantly, the implications of the words – sink in.

Today, we are immersed in a culture that has been deeply impacted by the Christian worldview. An example of this is if I were to share that as a family we sponsor two children, regularly give to charity and respond to ad hoc needs, you wouldn't be surprised, as we are used to charitable giving. Our 'junk' mail, magazines and TV adverts are full of inspirational, heartbreaking causes needing our financial support. Many of the great charities we unwittingly rely on as a country would close without support. What may be surprising is that this level of empathy was not 'the norm' in the pre-Christian pagan world.

Jesus' teaching that His followers were to love their enemies and show mercy to all was revolutionary in His day, and, to be honest, is radical today. In pagan culture, compassion for the needy was often regarded as foolish. When people gave gifts, they tended to be conditional gifts with the expectation that something such as public honour and recognition would be given in return.

Then along came Christianity, and culture began to change

History tells us Christianity spread rapidly during the first three centuries in the face of opposition and persecution. Experts think that there were probably no more than a few thousand Christians in AD 40, but by AD 300 they represented 10 per cent of the Roman Empire, approximately six million people, and by AD 350 that figure was more than thirty million.[5] This is an eyewatering level of growth. How fantastic would it be if Christianity began to grow at that level again? Churches needing to reopen, multiple services taking place throughout the week and every seat being taken. Picture the wave of love that would sweep through the land.

[5] Rodney Stark, 1996, *The Rise of Christianity: A Sociologist Reconsiders History* (Princeton, NJ: Princeton University Press, 1996), pp. 7-10.

Visualise with me Christians in prominent, influential positions in every sector, speaking positively into the lives of those they come into contact with. Let's take a minute to send an arrow prayer for revival (but minus the opposition and persecution if that is possible!).

If the experts are correct and by AD 350 there were more than thirty million Christians in the Roman Empire, this would have accounted for just over 50 per cent of the population. We have the Bible; we know these Christians were far from perfect, but our God is awe-inspiring and can use whatever we give Him to grow His kingdom and populate heaven.

Sociologist Rodney Stark credits the Christian ethic of compassion and care as being a major factor for this growth and paints a bleak picture of the misery and brutality of life in the urban Greco-Roman world:

> To cities filled with the homeless and impoverished, Christianity offered charity as well as hope. To cities filled with newcomers and strangers, Christianity offered an immediate basis for attachments. To cities filled with orphans and widows, Christianity provided a new and expanded sense of family. To cities torn by violent ethnic strife, Christianity offered a new basis for social solidarity. And to cities faced with epidemics, fires and earthquakes, Christianity offered effective nursing services.[6]

In a world where infanticide and child abandonment were defended by influential intellectuals such as Aristotle, Cicero and Seneca, Christians stepped in and got their

---

[6] Stark, *The Rise of Christianity*, p. 161.

hands dirty saving, rescuing and loving unwanted children.

As a child, one of my favourite cartoons was about a tall, skinny, white mouse called Danger Mouse and his sidekick, Penfold. This unlikely duo would get into all sorts of adventures but, without fail, Danger Mouse would leave unscathed after saving those who needed to be saved. The Danger Mouse theme tune was incredibly catchy and reinforced the belief that he would rescue those who were facing danger. This sounds like the early Christians.

Their response to need was radically countercultural and grounded in Jesus' teachings about human dignity and being made in God's image. It's impossible to know for every individual and situation, but I would guess their boldness was empowered by the Holy Spirit!

Long before Constantine legalised Christianity, the Church had created a system of social assistance, abundant generosity, that no pagan state had ever provided. The Church became the first organised institution of public welfare in Roman and Western history. In fact, Christians have done so much to shape the world we live in that one author has declared, 'A world from which the gospel had been banished would surely be one in which millions more of our fellows would go unfed, un-nursed, unsheltered and uneducated.'[7]

The emperor Julian the Apostate lamented that the Christians, whom he hated, showed love and compassion,

---

[7] David Bentley Hart, *Atheist Delusions: The Christian Revolution and Its Fashionable Enemies* (New Haven, CT: Yale University Press, 2009), p 16.

whereas his pagan countrymen did not. He famously stated, 'the impious Galileans support not only their own poor but ours as well'.[8]

Irrespective of the culture we find ourselves in, like our Christian ancestors we are called to a higher standard. Matthew 5:13-16 tells us we are called to be salt and light and to make an impact. We are called to be people of abundant, extravagant generosity.

Let's talk about time, talent and treasure

Our God is amazing, He is worthy of honour and He calls us to a lifetime of development, a lifetime of growth because He loves us too much to leave us as we are. We are to become less, and He is to become more.[9] Because of who He is, He is worthy of us giving extravagantly of our time, talent and treasure. If we look at these individually:

Time is self-explanatory – a giving of our personal time invested in something that will benefit others.

Talent – the ways we identify and deploy our talents for the benefit of others.

Treasure – how we give extravagantly from what we own.

Written like this, time, talent and treasure seem fairly ineffectual. However, to help bring them to life and to showcase the power they can wield, I'm going to share a

---

[8] christianhistoryinstitute.org/magazine/article/the-undeserving-poor (accessed 29th June 2023).
[9] See John the Baptist's words in John 3:30.

few stories. We're still back in time, and I want to encourage you to look for the time, talent and treasure in each of the stories below. Let's start with Basil of Caesarea.

Basil lived in what is now Turkey, from AD 329 to 379, and was a prominent, successful and gifted law teacher. When he became a Christian, his life was turned around and took on new meaning, and he gave away his personal family inheritance to help the poor. He stopped being a teacher of the law and became a sower of the seed. As a church leader in Caesarea, he organised a soup kitchen and distributed food during a famine that came on the heels of a drought. Serving food wasn't the most prestigious of roles for a man in the ancient world and was a humongous social demotion from being a lawyer.

Basil no longer cared about earthly expectations and spent his time working to rehabilitate thieves and prostitutes, and used his legal knowledge to challenge public officials if they failed to administer justice. Every morning and evening he could be found sharing the Word of God to large congregations. In addition to all his other activities, Basil supervised the building of a huge complex which included a poorhouse, hospice and hospital.

Where was the time, talent, and treasure?

A more modern example is Thomas Jones (1752-1845), who was a Welsh clergyman. Thomas was driven away from his parish church in Wales in 1785 because his parishioners were embarrassed by his 'enthusiasm'. Eventually he became curate of a tiny hamlet of forty-six houses in Northamptonshire and ministered faithfully for forty-three years.

From that humble base he transformed the surrounding community. He wrote devotional books in English and Welsh with all the profits being ploughed into charitable enterprises. He was the founder of Sunday schools, elementary ('Dame') schools, Sick Clubs and Clothing Clubs; he built six alms houses for aged widows; he founded an Education Society which enabled fifty evangelical laymen to enter the ministry. He created a wonderfully named 'Society for Poor Pious Clergymen' and he managed to raise funds to distribute more than £35,000 to clergy more needy than himself – his annual stipend was £25.

Did you see the time, talent and treasure?

One last example. History tells us modern nursing dates to the pioneering practice of an order of Lutheran deaconesses in Northern Germany in 1836. This seems like a bold claim but becomes even bolder when we read that it all started with Pastor Theodor Fliedner who gave refuge to one poor, sick and destitute prisoner and nursed him in his own home. Pastor Theodor then established a hospital with a hundred beds and trained poor women as nurses. His hospital and the professional care given became so famous throughout Europe that by the middle of the twentieth century, there were more than 35,000 deaconesses serving in parishes, schools, hospitals and prisons throughout the world.

In all three examples the time, talent and treasure of individuals aided by God was revolutionary and world-changing.

Can you see the higher standard that Jesus calls us to?

Generosity is fascinating, and some of us are better at it than others, although we all have the potential to be superstars in this area. However, sometimes we need to adapt our expectations. An example of this was when I shared at a Christian Union event in a prestigious London university. I was advised dinner would be provided, and was looking forward to what would be served. When it arrived, 'dinner' was individual cereal boxes with milk poured straight into the box, with the cereal being eaten from tiny wooden spoons. To a middle-aged woman, this doesn't constitute dinner. But to the students who attended, this was a stupendous, tasty and generous meal, with many having second and third helpings. In this scenario I needed to adapt, enlarge and contextualise my expectation of generosity.

While generosity comes in many guises and differing amounts, whether it can be called generosity is dependent on what it has cost the giver. A general overview of generosity could be described as the willingness to do kind things or to share what we have freely. This description sits comfortably with the responses I received to the survey question, 'How would you describe generosity?', the important addition being those who responded to the survey recognised and acknowledged the influence of God alongside the desire to enhance the well-being of the receiver in obedience to God.

Here are some of the survey responses describing the vast subject that is generosity:

Giving sacrificially when you see a need or are inspired by God to give.

Being obedient with what God has given you in its fullest sense.

Giving what God has given you to bless or help someone else.

Unexpectedly giving to others to meet a need or bring a blessing.

Recognising everything we have is God-given and using the money you have to bless others.

A natural part of the Christian life.

Giving to God and giving to others out of the blessing we have been given.

A recognition of all that God has given and a desire to be part of His provision to others.

Seeking the smile of God.

A recognition of all that God has given me and a desire to be part of His provision to others.

Giving away freely from the good that God has given to me for the sake of others, and for His glory.

That God plays such a prominent part in some of the responses isn't a surprise, as those who answered the survey question 'practising generosity is an important part of the Christian discipleship journey' unanimously responded that yes, it is.

Dream with me for a minute and imagine a world where every believer is outrageously generous with what they have; what a world it would be! With more funds to provide additional resources, how would your church and church family benefit? Possibly more outreaches impacting those in the local community, a bigger building, extra staff? Maybe none of these would suffice because God has something bigger, better and new for you, something you are currently unable to dream or imagine.

Coming back to the description of generosity, some responses didn't specifically name God but had His generosity at the heart of the response. Here are a few examples:

Giving in a way that falls outside what the person expects or asks.

Going above and beyond to help those who need you.

Being generous with words, time, skills, abilities and finance.

Giving without counting the cost.

It's an attitude first, and an action second. It starts in the heart and travels to the head and gut!

A practical demonstration of love.

Giving beyond obligation.

While reading through these responses I felt humbled and grateful to be part of a community with generosity at its core. I also felt challenged to explore my own motivations for generosity, and must admit they are not always pure.

On reflection, I realised I am not wholly selfless in my giving and am more likely to give to a cause or a person where I'll feel an element of satisfaction. This may be because I immediately see the benefit of my gift or it's a cause close to my heart. Either way, the essence of who I am, unless I receive a nudge from God, will always steer my generosity. As God has made me, knows me and continues to guide me, I am comfortable with this revelation, with the caveat that my will never overrides His.

For most of us, we probably don't need more than a few seconds to remember an act of generosity enacted, directed or witnessed within the last few months.

Question 10 of the survey I circulated asked for stories of generosity. Here are a few of the responses:

Early days of marriage we wanted to get on housing ladder but had no deposit. One day I met an old lady in need and gave the money in my pocket £20 which I really needed. That night a knock on the door and some friends came in and gave us £3K towards a deposit. The next day someone else offered a £3K interest free loan; £6K is what we needed back then and were able to secure a mortgage! God is faithful.

I have been the recipient of others' generosity over the years both practically and financially. Many years ago, when the Poll Tax was in force, I didn't have enough money to pay it one month. I hadn't mentioned this to anyone but an envelope was popped through my door with the exact amount in cash inside.

It's God's attention to detail that always gets me more than the amounts. Our daughter's wedding was happening and we were £400 short to make the final payment to the music group doing the reception. We had to pay the band in cash. As the week leading up to the wedding went on, we still didn't have any funds. We didn't tell anyone, just kept

31

praying. On the day before the wedding, I came home at lunchtime and found an envelope through the door – in it was £400... in cash! If it had been a cheque, we couldn't have banked it in time to get the cash out – so God provided in cash.

I love these stories of generosity; they warm my heart and make me smile. We know God is interested in every aspect of our lives and, for me, these stories are concrete proof of that fact.

A mantra that almost every fundraiser I know practises is that 'generosity breeds generosity'. When we see someone doing something good, an act that benefits another, whether it's logical or illogical, it encourages us to do the same. We see this in 1 Chronicles 29:2-5 where David tells those assembled:

> With all my resources I have provided for the temple of my God – gold for the gold work, silver for the silver, bronze for the bronze, iron for the iron and wood for the wood, as well as onyx for the settings, turquoise, stones of various colours, and all kinds of fine stone and marble – all of these in large quantities. Besides, in my devotion to the temple of my God I now give my personal treasures of gold and silver for the temple of my God, over and above everything I have provided for this holy temple: three thousand talents of gold (gold of Ophir) and seven thousand talents of refined silver, for the overlaying of the walls of the buildings, for the gold work and the silver work, and for all the work to be done by the craftsmen.

Then he issues the challenge:

> Now, who is willing to consecrate themselves to the
> LORD today?

The challenge was big, and so was the response as
everyone generously gave materials that could be used to
build the temple. And the giving didn't end there, as we
read in verse 21:

> The next day they made sacrifices to the LORD and
> presented burnt offerings to him: a thousand bulls,
> a thousand rams and a thousand male lambs,
> together with their drink offerings, and other
> sacrifices in abundance for all Israel.

Generosity is contagious

Generosity often spreads and infects others, which has the
potential to impact individuals, churches, communities,
counties, even a nation for the glory of God. That's
something I want to be part of!

It even has the potential to impact us. In our efforts to
be generous givers, moving beyond our comfort zone and
giving sacrificially, we demonstrate and deepen our trust
in God to provide for our need.

To finish this chapter, I want to share a personal story
that happened recently. This story doesn't particularly
show me in a good light, but it does highlight the wisdom
and love of our heavenly Father.

The story begins following a long, nine-hour train
journey, where I departed from the train on to the
platform in a terrible mood. I was tired, hungry and

desperate to get home to my husband and children. It felt like every person walking in front of me was part sloth and had decided that they would all take it in turns to block my way and slow my journey. I had another train to catch, the clock was ticking and I was fighting against the urge to use my suitcase as a path-clearing bulldozer. None of this made me happy and, with a face like a camel eating a lemon, and an attitude to match, I exited the train station and heard a busker singing the Bethel song 'Goodness of God'.[10] If you're not familiar with this song, part of the lyrics talk about God's goodness and how we respond by surrendering to Him, laying down our life and giving Him our all. Powerfully challenging words.

Hearing this song stopped me in my tracks. I forgot about the train I needed to catch, the gnawing feeling in my stomach and the sloth-like fellow travellers as I was struck by God's amazing, limitless and unwarranted generosity. The lyrics in this song refocused me, the light contained in these words melted away the darkness that was surrounding and within me. My gratitude to God spilled out in me being financially generous to the busker who had taken the time to share God's love through worship.

As I don't believe in coincidence, I wholeheartedly believe this was God's providence. I know I wouldn't have been the only person who benefited from the busker and the songs he was singing, but I do believe that my heavenly Father, who gives good, generous gifts, delighted in giving me the gift of peace that evening.

---

[10] Bethel Music and Jenn Johnson. From the album *Victory* (2019).

Questions

- As mentioned, in the survey that was circulated, the average score relating to how generous each participant rated themselves was 7.32. What score would you give yourself and why?

- How do you use your time, talent and treasure? Was there a particular story that impacted you?

- Do you believe practising generosity is an important part of the Christian discipleship journey? Why do you believe this and where (if anywhere) do you see it being lived out?

- There is a long list of responses to the question, 'How would you describe generosity?' Is there a response that resonates with you? How would you answer this question in your own words?

- As you think back over your own experiences, what act of generosity stands out for you? How do you understand 'generosity breeds generosity'?

2

Money, Money, Money

Now we've dipped our toe into generosity, I want us to delve into the topic of money. At this point I want to stress that I do not see money or being wealthy as bad things. If you have a bulging wallet and a healthy bank balance, if you own your own home and drive your own car, I believe this is because God has blessed you in this way; that is a good thing. God blesses different people in different ways and with some the blessing comes in the form of finance. Money has the potential to enhance, bless and bring goodness. I see this in my work almost every day. This is the good side, the healthy side of money.

The other side

Conversely, we've all heard and seen the trappings it can bring when our relationship, possession and need of it has an unhealthy hold on us, which reminds me of the fictional story of a very rich businessman who was near death and desperate to retain his riches. After much pleading, he was eventually given special permission to bring one suitcase with him to heaven. Overjoyed, the businessman gathered his largest suitcase, filled it with pure gold bars and placed it beside his bed. Upon his death, the man showed up at the Pearly Gates where he was greeted by St Peter who insisted on opening the suitcase to inspect the worldly items that the businessman found too precious to leave behind. As the lid sprang back to reveal the gold, St Peter exclaimed, 'You brought pavement?'[11]

This man, and the challenge and regret he faced when he thought about letting go of the wealth he had accumulated, are things we can probably all relate to. Most of us will have an item that we have bought or has been bought for us that we don't want to let go of. In our minds this item's importance, whether it's a car, jewellery, house or gold bars, can be magnified beyond its actual value and take an unhealthy hold over us. The way we view this item can become distorted.

A quick question – if I were to fill a normal-sized pint glass with water and ask you to guess how much it weighed, what would your answer be? Would you guess one ounce? Maybe even two ounces? Perhaps you'd be a bit more conservative and guess below these two figures.

If you've taken this seriously and have gone to the trouble of filling a glass and weighing it, what comes next will really annoy you. The weight of the glass is immaterial; what counts is how long we hold on to it. If we hold it for a minute or two, it's fairly light. If we hold the glass for an hour our arm may start to ache. If we hold it for a whole day, the likelihood is our arm will begin to

---

[11] This is a popular fictional story, source unknown, referring to Revelation 21:21: 'The twelve gates were twelve pearls, each gate made of a single pearl. The great street of the city was of gold, as pure as transparent glass.'

cramp, eventually forcing us to drop the glass and its contents on to the floor. The weight of the glass doesn't change, but the longer we hold it, the heavier a burden it becomes. The longer we hold on to it, the greater the importance we place on it. The more it becomes the centre of everything we think and do.

We can face the same danger with money and what it affords. In some versions of Scripture, this is referred to as mammon.[12] Mammon stands in opposition to God. It wants to rule, control and consume and forms part of the 'rulers ... authorities ... powers' that Paul speaks out about so strongly in Ephesians 6:12 and Colossians 1:16. Mammon can be summarised as the pursuit of worldly things and earthly desires that divert our attention and love from God. This is why Jesus tells us, 'No one can serve two masters. Either you will hate the one and love the other, or you will be devoted to the one and despise the other. You cannot serve both God and Money' (Matthew 6:24).

As Martin Luther wisely observed when talking about living an obedient Christian life, 'There are three conversions necessary: the conversion of the heart, mind and the purse.'[13] This book seeks to engage in the latter conversion but indisputably all are interlinked and flow from each other.

Several decades ago, while I was walking to our local shop to purchase ice creams for an after-dinner treat, two men pushed me to the ground and demanded I hand over

---

[12] For example, KJV, NKJV.
[13] Martin Luther, quoted in Edward W Bauman, *Where Your Treasure Is* (Arlington, VA: Bauman Bible Tele casts, 1980), p 74.

my purse which contained around £5. Money was incredibly scarce and my purse was beautiful, red, heart-shaped and had been an extravagant present from my husband. The men were desperate and meant business, but I loved that purse, which led me to clutching it close to my chest and screaming, 'Help!' Despite a slight escalation in threats and violence, this encounter ended with the two men fleeing and my purse remaining safely in my hands. In hindsight this seems ridiculous, but people take all types of crazy risks in the pursuit of money. A fascination with money abounds, and it's no surprise when we acknowledge the spirit of mammon coupled with the fact that we need money to eat, sleep comfortably (beds cost money!), buy clothes and generally live.

For some, money is the heartbeat, rhythm and driver of life. It is the reason they get out of bed in the morning, it determines their career choices, where they live, even how many children they'll have – I know of people who refused to have more offspring as the cost of that additional ticket was the difference between flying business or economy. To an extent I can understand this, as during my time working in finance, how much I could earn determined my choice of roles and employers.

I don't want to spend too much time exploring the negative aspects of money as that isn't the purpose of this book. What I hope I've re-emphasised is that there is a spiritual battle when it comes to finance; we have to choose between selfless or selfish, to learn to trust in God or rely on ourselves. We also need to apply godly wisdom, which we'll look at later.

Money also shines a light in to the deepest part of our soul

It offers lessons on things like risk, happiness and faith.

Recently I read about a Liverpudlian researcher, David Clarke, who handed over his £100K inheritance to a group of twelve strangers to distribute how they wished, as long as it fell within the remits of tackling poverty within the L8 postcode of Liverpool. His reasoning behind this was that he already had enough money and didn't need any more. What a lovely, kind-hearted, generous man![14] Not to the same extent as David Clarke, but almost every day we need to make choices based on how much money we have and where we want, or need, to spend it. Because of this, it remains a common denominator that links us together.

People from different generations, born on different continents, into different families, experiencing different job markets will have a different understanding and relationship with money that will shape how they pursue, save and spend it. At the very least, almost every human on earth will use, spend and possibly save money.

My nan and grandad were born during the First World War and raised a family through and following the Second World War. Neither was born into a wealthy family and they knew what it was like to go without, to have second-hand clothing (before it became trendy to do so), to make food last and to literally not have a penny to their name.

I was born just before the financial boom of the mid and late 1980s which saw favourable economic conditions for

---

[14] www.theguardian.com/uk-news/2024/feb/07/liverpool-man-who-inherited-100000-lets-12-strangers-give-the-money-away (accessed 27th February 2024).

my family. My dad had his own limited company and the business was doing well. Throughout my childhood I never experienced need or had to worry about finances.

My grandparents shared with me what it was like to have a lack of money, to eat whatever was available, to feed a family through rationing and to worry about how the next bill would be paid. I received this information through them; I didn't live through their experience, which means I don't have their emotional scars or fears. My childhood, those early formative years, were vastly different from those of my grandparents – different generation, different time in history, different experiences. This left me with a different relationship with money.

Money means different things to different people. Former child star, actress and model Brooke Shields is quoted as stating, 'I'm so naive about finances. Once my mother mentioned an amount and I realized I didn't understand, she had to explain, "That's like three Mercedes." Then I understood.'[15]

This type of comparison would be incomprehensible for a family or individual where food is scarce. If we're not careful, we can judge those who have a different financial worldview.

Whether my shop of choice is Lidl or Waitrose, my favourite brand is a budget one or a so-called luxury brand, I shop when I know the stock will be marked down because of dates or I shop at my convenience, I am fortunate to have a choice. In 2019 I visited a number of families who lived in various Kenyan slums; this choice is

---

[15] www.humorliving.com/funny-money-quotes/ (accessed 21st July 2023).

not available to them, and to even have such a choice would be viewed as a luxury. Different generations, geographical locations, expectations and family situations equal a different relationship with money. The distinction comes in the differing amounts, which equals a vastly diverse experience and impacts our relationship and attitude towards it. A great example of this involves one of America's most-loved presidents.

John F Kennedy grew up in one of the wealthiest American families, and while running for president he was asked what he remembered from the Great Depression, during which he would have been a teenager and young adult. At this point the Depression was reputed to be the worst economic downturn in the history of the industrialised world; at its lowest point, some 15 million Americans were unemployed and nearly half the country's banks had failed. John F Kennedy responded, 'No, I have no memory of it at all, really, except what I read in history books. My experience was the war; that's what I remember, but the Depression had no effect on me.'[16]

John F Kennedy's experience of the Great Depression was second-hand; it left no scars, but for others it was life-changing. Many went into the Depression with a relationship with money that changed radically as they were faced with the reality of poverty. John F Kennedy had no such experience.

Morgan Housel, in his book *The Psychology of Money*, highlights this when he writes that every person's

[16] www.jfklibrary.org/asset-viewer/archives/jfkoh-hss-01 (accessed 10th July 2023).

experience with money represents 0.00000001 per cent of the world's experience with money, but to that one person, it represents 80 per cent of how the financial world works.[17]

In all likelihood this was true for my grandparents, Brooke Shields, John F Kennedy, and it is true for me and you.

For lots of people, money is personal before it is anything else

It is ours, kept in our account, viewed as our possession that we have worked hard for and earned. In reality, we are only ever stewards of the money God gifts us, but it can be easy to lose sight of this.

As a young woman in my mid-twenties, I worked for a well-known high street bank advising wealthy clients how to attribute their funds and maximise the return. Some of these clients were multi-millionaires, others were not quite in that category, but all of those I advised had more funds than me. I remember one particular client forgetting he had an account containing just over £1 million and another buying a helicopter for a charity to offset his tax liability.

I loved my job and I loved meeting with my clients. Sitting with them, discussing their financial dreams and aspirations, provided a glimpse into another world. It was a world I had never inhabited. A world full of six-figure bonuses, multiple holiday homes, expensive sports cars, numerous staff and incredibly healthy bank accounts. However, each person I met was unique, managing their

[17] Morgan Housel, *The Psychology of Money* (Hampshire: Harriman House, 2020), p 9.

personal history, distinctive view of the world, generosity and finances in a way that worked for them. I didn't always share their outlook on finance, but every encounter helped enlarge my experience and increase my perspective.

As you read through this book, I want to challenge you to put aside any thoughts you have about what others give, to stop measuring yourself against them and to assess your situation in its own vacuum. What others have is ultimately irrelevant; it's what you have been given from God and what you choose to do with it that's important.

For many of us, and possibly as a result of media coverage, we often relate an excess of money to increased influence. And this can be true; however, we know it isn't always the case, as many of those who responded to the survey named the story of the poor widow's offering as their favourite Bible story about financial generosity:

> Jesus sat down opposite the place where the offerings were put and watched the crowd putting their money into the temple treasury. Many rich people threw in large amounts. But a poor widow came and put in two very small copper coins, worth only a few pence.
>
> Calling his disciples to him, Jesus said, 'Truly I tell you, this poor widow has put more into the treasury than all the others. They all gave out of their wealth; but she, out of her poverty, put in everything – all she had to live on.'
> (Mark 12:41-44)

We've just read that others in the crowd gave bigger amounts to the temple treasury that would have had a much wider reach than the widow's two copper coins. So why is this recounting of a poor widow's offering – a woman who would have held no power – had the most influence for those that responded to the survey? I believe it's because her gift cost her. It didn't come out of surplus; it was literally all she had. In all likelihood, those two copper coins were the only things standing between her and hunger. But by faith and in an act of loving worship she returned them to the hands of God.

Money can be used to worship and raise up the name of Jesus. As pastor, speaker and author Bill Johnson has said, every dollar (insert your own currency here) that is given to God is a soldier in His army.[18]

Entertainment

I've just alluded to the media as being influential, but so is the world of entertainment.

I want to suggest that without us being aware, we have been influenced by what we have read, watched and heard. Turning our eyes in this direction for a moment leaves us spoiled for choice in the search of an enlarged and diverse worldview.

Over the years there have been so many songs about money. They range from 'Brother, Can You Spare a Dime?' by Bing Crosby that became a soundtrack to the Great

---

[18] This was said at the Catch The Fire twentieth anniversary in Toronto, Canada, January 2014. Catch the Fire Church in Toronto is the flagship church of the global, non-denominational Catch the Fire World ministry. See www.ctftoronto.com (accessed 11th April 2024).

Depression, to the iconic ABBA dreaming and singing of money and a wealthy man therefore negating the need to work and earn a salary, right through to the more explicit song by Travie McCoy and Bruno Mars titled 'Billionaire' listing all the ways life would be different if they were billionaires.

Our obsession with money doesn't end with singing, but also encompasses the big screen with many films having money and the accumulation of it being a central theme. Think *The Wolf of Wall Street*, based on the true story of risk-taking Wall Street stockbroker Jordan Belfort who amasses a huge amount of wealth. Or any one of the *Oceans* series about a skilled band of thieves headed up by George Clooney who, through working together, steal something of great worth from someone who, the plot leads us to believe, probably didn't deserve to own it in the first place.

Television has also tapped into our interest in money, with numerous quiz-type programmes where contestants face multiple choice questions, normally banking an increasing amount of funds for each correct answer.

If we were passing each other in the street and I leaned in and said, 'This time next year we'll be millionaires,' you might think I was crazy, but you'd probably recognise this as the mantra Del Boy from *Only Fools and Horses* used to say on a regular basis.

The reason that money infiltrates everything and everywhere is because money taps deeply into our psyche, it's part of our everyday life and has been so for thousands of years. Aristotle, who was an ancient Greek philosopher and scientist and credited as being one of the greatest intellectual figures of Western history, said about money:

> To give away money is an easy matter and in any man's power. But to decide to whom to give it and how large and when, and for what purpose and how, is neither in every man's power nor an easy matter.[19]

For thousands of years, acquiring money has been a source of battles and blessings, and for this we have to thank King Alyattes. In 600 BC, Lydia's King Alyattes minted what is believed to have been the first official currency, the Lydian stater. Today, when someone says 'as rich as Croesus', they are referring to the last Lydian king, who minted the first gold coin.

We have come a long way since then. The total value of all the money in the world is estimated to be around $418 trillion, a figure that would make King Alyattes' eyes water. In a recent article, Forbes puts the number of billionaires in the world at 2,668,[20] though this is a very small number compared to the 7.837 billion people who currently call earth their home.

While most of us will not personally know a billionaire, we will, through the power of the media, be able to name at least one. Whether we like it or not, money, and those who have it, tend to gain our respect and interest. This may be because they are genuinely nice, talented and interesting, or because money equals power and privilege.

---

[19] Cited in Patricia Illingworth, Thomas Pogge and Leif Wenar, eds, *Giving Well: The Ethics of Philanthropy* (Oxford: Oxford University Press, 2011), p 3.

[20] www.forbes.com/sites/chasewithorn/2022/04/05/forbes-36th-annual-worlds-billionaires-list-facts-and-figures-2022/ (accessed 19th June 2023).

Possibly it's because those with significant amounts of money are in the minority and are therefore viewed as a curiosity. We may often wonder what it would be like to purchase whatever we desire, travel wherever we want, live in a bigger home and have our own swimming pool.

Whatever the reason, money has always grabbed our attention. Jesus understood this and didn't shy away from addressing the subject, with thirteen of the thirty-nine parables in the Gospels talking about money. Jesus knew mentioning money, an element that could mean the difference between eating or starving, living or dying, connected with the reality of His listeners.

But, as is often the case, the headlines don't tell the whole story.

Jesus did talk a lot about money, there's no debating that. However, at times Jesus was simply using money to demonstrate a bigger point. What I mean by this is He was not really teaching about money, but rather using it as an illustration His audience would be able to grasp and understand.

A great example of this can be found in Matthew 20:1-16:

> For the kingdom of heaven is like a landowner who went out early in the morning to hire workers for his vineyard. He agreed to pay them a denarius for the day and sent them into his vineyard.
>
> About nine in the morning he went out and saw others standing in the market-place doing nothing. He told them, 'You also go and work in my vineyard, and I will pay you whatever is right.' So they went.

He went out again about noon and about three in the afternoon and did the same thing. About five in the afternoon he went out and found still others standing around. He asked them, 'Why have you been standing here all day long doing nothing?'

'Because no one has hired us,' they answered.

He said to them, 'You also go and work in my vineyard.'

When evening came, the owner of the vineyard said to his foreman, 'Call the workers and pay them their wages, beginning with the last ones hired and going on to the first.'

The workers who were hired about five in the afternoon came and each received a denarius. So when those came who were hired first, they expected to receive more. But each one of them also received a denarius. When they received it, they began to grumble against the landowner. 'These who were hired last worked only one hour,' they said, 'and you have made them equal to us who have borne the burden of the work and the heat of the day.'

But he answered one of them, 'I am not being unfair to you, friend. Didn't you agree to work for a denarius? Take your pay and go. I want to give the one who was hired last the same as I gave you. Don't I have the right to do what I want with my own money? Or are you envious because I am generous?'

So the last will be first, and the first will be last.'

In this portion of Scripture, Jesus tells a story about the payment of vineyard workers. I want to suggest that Jesus isn't teaching about business practices or how to annoy those who work in Human Resources. Instead, He's giving us a glimpse of the grace that abounds in God's kingdom and uses money as a means that others, irrespective of what century they have been born in, can grasp and understand.

Whether we like it or not, money and our interaction with it has shaped the world we live in and the way we live. For some, money will have a strong hold on them; for others, the grip will be loose, but none of us will have escaped its influence.

Questions

- Take a moment to consider your money story. What is your history and your present relationship with money that shapes the way you approach saving, spending and being generous?

- Can you identify with the phrase 'the pursuit of wealth'?

- How has your relationship and expectations of money been shaped by songs, TV and films?

- Do you agree with Aristotle when he said, 'To give away money is an easy matter and in any man's power. But to decide to whom to give it and how large and when, and for what purpose and how, is neither in every man's power nor an easy matter.' Is there any part of this quote that you find challenging?

- Ask yourself, who do you know and what conversations could you have that would enlarge your financial worldview?

3

The Beauty of Unity

Back in 1991 on a normal day in California, there was such a loud crash that people in the nearby towns speculated there had been a big train accident. They later found out that this was no train accident but the Dyerville Giant, a redwood tree measuring 362 feet tall, making it taller than the Statue of Liberty, falling to the earth.

Such was the impact of this giant tree toppling over that pieces of the redwood were found 500 feet away, and the disturbance was registered on a nearby seismograph, a device scientists use to measure earthquakes.[21]

I'm sharing this because redwood trees are pretty amazing. They can live for more than a thousand years and grow so tall their top is out of sight. You would think that such a tall tree would need deep roots to keep it stable, but the roots only extend down six to twelve feet, which doesn't seem substantial enough for a tree that soars hundreds of feet into the air.

The first time I read this, I immediately asked myself, 'How are they able to live so long and grow so tall without

---

[21] education.nationalgeographic.org/resource/tall-trees (accessed 21st July 2023).

toppling? How have they survived earthquakes, landslides, floods, strong winds and other trees falling against them?'

The answer is simple: they thrive and survive in the same way we do, by staying connected and living in community.

The root systems of these ancient trees spread outwards up to a hundred feet from the trunk and are robustly intertwined with the roots of other redwood trees, enhancing their stability and increasing their growth potential. To put it simply, because of their connection to each other they are stronger.

When Christians are connected, combining God-given giftings, skills and blessings, we are stronger, better equipped and able to achieve more. Just like the redwood trees, our connection to each other means we can collectively soar higher.

Ecclesiastes 4:9-12 talks about friendship and tells us:

Two are better than one,
because they have a good return for their labour:
if either of them falls down,
one can help the other up.
But pity anyone who falls
and has no one to help them up.
Also, if two lie down together, they will keep warm.
But how can one keep warm alone?
Though one may be overpowered,
two can defend themselves.
A cord of three strands is not quickly broken.

The power of friendship, the sheer magnetism of being part of a friendship, is everywhere we look. We read about it; I can't think of one fictional book I've ever read that hasn't had the theme of friendship running through it. We enjoy seeing it bloom on reality TV programmes and lived out in series.

Most of us will have watched or be aware of the TV series *Friends*. This slightly addictive and amazingly successful programme which ran from 1994 to 2004, and centred on the lives of six New Yorkers, was still the favourite TV programme for young people in the UK in 2019.[22] In 2019, Sky One aired a *Friends* reunion; this was the most-watched show on Sky One ever.[23] Such is the allure of friendship.

Many films also use the power of friendship to make us laugh, cry and feel a whole range of emotions as we see friends journey together, take risks for each other and be there through the highs and the lows, accepting each other for who they are.

And as Christians, the knowledge and understanding that friendship, being connected on a deeper level with one another, is compelling shouldn't come as a surprise. Scripture shows us, from Genesis to Revelation, that we were made to be connected. As my friend Phil says, 'We are hardwired in our bodies for connection,'[24] to such an

[22] www.bbc.co.uk/news/education-47043831 (accessed 28th July 2023).
[23] www.skygroup.sky/en-gb/article/the-one-where-friends-the-reunion-becomes-sky-one-s-most-watched-show-ever (accessed 28th July 2023).
[24] Phil Knox, *The Best of Friends* (London: IVP, 2023), pp 9-11 includes wider context.

extent that it is healthier to eat a kebab with friends than a salad alone.[25]

The ultimate relationship

If we turn to Scripture, we can immediately see a glimpse of the ultimate relationship, the Holy Trinity, one being, acting and relating as three persons.

The first example we have of this amazing unity is in Genesis 1:1 where it declares, 'In the beginning God created the heavens and the earth.' But we know God was not alone, as almost immediately afterwards we read that 'the Spirit of God was hovering over the waters' (Genesis 1:2). The book of John tells us, 'In the beginning was the Word' (John 1:1). The Word, as we know, is Jesus. These scriptures allow a glimpse into the wonder and accord of the Holy Trinity.

When we put these scriptures together along with others in the Old and New Testament, we get a picture of Father, Son and Holy Spirit working together; we see the ultimate relationship. We see unity personified.

From the moment humankind was created and blessed by God (Genesis 1:28), He has wanted us to be in relationship with Him and each other. God regularly walked with Adam, the first man, in the Garden of Eden, and created Eve to be Adam's companion. He gave us the ability to have children, to build families. He filled us with the Holy Spirit and created the Church. All fantastic ways for us to form friendships, build unity and not be alone.

We are made in God's image, and just as the Father, Son and Holy Spirit live in relationship with each other, we

---

[25] Knox, *The Best of Friends*, p 12.

have been designed to do the same. If you are harbouring doubts about your need to rub shoulders with your fellow man or woman, Genesis 2:18 refutes this by asserting, 'It is not good for the man to be alone.'

In the church I co-pastor with my husband, I teach the teens. We always start with a really simple exercise where we all share one good and one bad thing about our week. We call this POMROS (Puddle Of Mud, Ray Of Sunshine). We do this because as well as learning more about God and going deeper in our faith, I want all of us to learn more about each other and go deeper in our friendships. It's almost impossible to be a good, consistent friend to another person if they remain a stranger. For friendship to grow, there needs to be a sacrifice of time, an element of trust and a willingness to attach our roots.

But when looking at generosity, friendship alone isn't our ultimate destination, it's our springboard, our foundation, and opens the door to take us to the next level, which is love.

Throughout the Bible we find so many examples and explanations of how to love. There are individual love stories such as Ruth and Boaz (and Ruth and Naomi), David and Jonathan, and the daughter of Pharoah and the infant Moses. Not all of these 'loves', of course, are romantic.

In 1 Corinthian 13:4-7 we are told what love looks like:

Love is patient, love is kind. It does not envy, it does not boast, it is not proud. It does not dishonour others, it is not self-seeking, it is not easily angered, it keeps no record of wrongs. Love does not delight in evil but rejoices with the truth. It always protects, always trusts, always hopes, always perseveres.

But it doesn't end there; with God there is always more. We are told that in addition to loving one another, as believers we are all one body, linked together, responsible for each other, despite having individual roles to play.[26] Jesus builds upon this when He prays:

> My prayer is not for them alone. I pray also for those who will believe in me through their message, that all of them may be one, Father, just as you are in me and I am in you. May they also be in us so that the world may believe that you have sent me. I have given them the glory that you gave me, that they may be one as we are one— I in them and you in me – so that they may be brought to complete unity. Then the world will know that you sent me and have loved them even as you have loved me.
> (John 17:20-23)

This is a high calling, but one that as children who are united to Christ, we are capable of fulfilling.

Being in 'complete unity' is more than just being friends

It's sharing godly love as a mirror of His glory.

When we love each other, feel connected to each other and view others as an extension of our own body in the ways Scripture has described, it becomes easier to act generously. We are no longer reliant on external

---

[26] 1 Corinthians 12:12-27; Romans 12:4-5.

motivators but can respond heart to heart, spirit to spirit with an open hand. Our neighbour becomes the person we love, regardless of geographical location. Friendship remains, but is fuelled by love and an understanding of unity.

Within my role as a fundraiser for a Christian charity, unity often finds expression in the gifting and receiving of money. It's the recognition that one part of the body has something that would greatly benefit another. There is no hierarchy in this transaction; it is an expression of love and distribution of funds with the sole aim of providing assistance. It allows us to enter another's world, to achieve things together that we could never do alone. Often, the most generous acts of financial unity that I've personally witnessed start with a prompting from the Holy Spirit and belief that everything we own belongs to God.

One of the most humbling examples of abundant and consistent generosity happened several years ago while on a family holiday in the Dominican Republic. We left the luxury of our hotel and drove to an area surrounded by sugar plantations where the average house had no running water and limited access to food. Many children were running about shoeless and barely clothed; poverty was evident wherever we looked. But so was love!

We met with the local school teacher who had lived in this slum (her words, not mine) for all her life, had taught the local children for just over forty years and knew everyone's family. She confided that she could have had a more comfortable, affluent life working in a different area in a better equipped school, but she felt called to stay, share and show love in this place. She shared with pride about the pupils she had taught and the success they had achieved as lawyers, teachers and numerous other vocations. Her colleague disclosed how most of what this teacher earned, which wasn't a huge amount, was poured back into the community. Love literally shone from this teacher's face and dripped from her every word. The financial sacrifice she had made and continued to make was real, generous and came at a personal cost that enabled others to have a better future.

Let us learn from Scripture and be people who act generously, live in unity, love abundantly and give sacrificially.

Questions

- How would you summarise friendship? How have your friendships influenced your life?

- Are there any similarities between the way you interact with others and the root structure of a redwood tree? What lessons can we take away?

- Are you aware of the triggers that tend to motivate your financial giving? Do you have a process that you follow?

- How easy is it to see the link between love, unity and generosity?

- What examples of generosity have made the biggest impact on you and how you live your life?

4

The Gift of a Generous Giver

There once was a strongman at a circus sideshow who demonstrated his power before large audiences every night.

Toward the end of one performance, he squeezed the juice from a lemon between his hands. He said to the onlookers, 'I will offer $200 to anyone here who can squeeze another drop from this lemon.'

A thin older lady hobbled up the stage. She picked up the lemon and clamped it between her two frail, boney hands. She squeezed. And out came a teaspoon of lemon juice.

The strongman was amazed. He paid the woman $200 but privately asked her, 'What is the secret of your strength?'

'Practice,' the woman answered. 'I have been treasurer of my church for forty-two years!'[27]

I know that is a bad joke and I apologise for subjecting you to it, although for some of you who are church treasurers

---

[27] www.anglicancompass.com/funny-you-said-that-stewardship-and-humor (accessed 11th April 2024).

or leaders, there may be an element of truth lurking behind the humour. If you're able to relate to the older lady in the story, you have my sympathy and prayers!

Over the years I have heard so many sermons on spiritual gifts, but never have I heard anyone preach on the gift of giving. In the culture we live in, where money is one of the last taboos, this is understandable, but conversely it is remarkable, as many of us talk about money and the cost of living every day. It's also astounding that this gift is not widely shared in a Christian setting, as not only would many of our churches, individuals and mission organisations suffer without this gift being exercised, but it is also mentioned in Romans 12:6-8:

> We have different gifts, according to the grace given to each of us. If your gift is prophesying, then prophesy in accordance with your faith; if it is serving, then serve; if it is teaching, then teach; if it is to encourage, then give encouragement; if it is giving, then give generously; if it is to lead, do it diligently; if it is to show mercy, do it cheerfully.

Three of these gifts are typically upfront gifts: prophecy,[28] teaching and leading. Many of us will be reasonably familiar with these gifts and will see at least one, if not all three gifts, at church every Sunday.

The remainder tend to be utilised behind the scenes: serving, encouraging, giving and mercy. They can be

---

[28] Prophecy is to declare a message from God to a nation, community or individual.

viewed as lesser gifts and definitely don't tend to receive as much attention, but they are invaluable.

While all are needed in the body of Christ and are interlinked, we are only going to touch on the gift of giving generously. John Rinehart refers to those moving in the gift of giving as believers who aren't content to be spectators but are instead backstage VIPs.[29]

In my experience, those with this gift tend to act on God's promises with confidence, demonstrating a high level of faith in His ability to overcome obstacles and do the miraculous. They view their finances through the lens of, 'How much money do I need to live on?' as opposed to, 'How much money do I need to give God?' They gift money thoughtfully, cheerfully, trusting in His provision and with a sense of moving forward in God's will. Some of those I've met who move in the gift of giving are resourceful, inspiring, disciplined and stewardship-minded.

Robert Morris expands upon this in his book *The Blessed Life*,[30] and lists the classic signs of a believer with the gift of giving. He suggests that as investors in the kingdom they want their gift to make a difference, can recognise manipulation, tend to have a strong grasp of the principles of finance, have a desire to feel appreciated and are 'wise investors that are attracted to strong leaders with a strong vision'. While this list is not exhaustive, I'm sure one or two individuals have immediately come to mind, people

---

[29] John Rinehart, *Gospel Patrons* (Scotts Valley, CA: CreateSpace Independent Publishing Platform, 2014), p 22.
[30] Robert Morris, *The Blessed Life* (Bloomington, MN: Bethany House Publishers), 2002.

who operate in this gift within your church family or wider community. Maybe you've recognised this gift, or the seed of this gift, in yourself.

Without fail, those individuals I have been blessed to come across who have the gift of giving generously always enthuse and motivate me with their selfless passion to build the Church, bless others and glorify God. These are people who will move forward and step out, when others are content to stand still. There have been numerous occasions when I have operated in this gift and there have been times when I have been on the receiving end of this gift; both have been humbling experiences.

For example, several years ago we rented a lovely farmhouse that belonged to a couple in the church we pastor. The farmhouse was big, surrounded by lots of land, and despite it being extremely rural (at that time we were more accustomed to urban areas), we felt that as a family we would be happy there. The only downside was no decorating had been done for fifty years! Two weeks before we moved in, we began to strip, clean and paint. We desperately needed new carpets but didn't have the funds for them and planned to go into our overdraft to purchase them. After shopping around extensively (we had no money and needed the best deal), we purchased carpets for the grand price of £1,500. We hadn't shared about the cost of the carpets or the need to plunder our overdraft, but just before the payment deadline, two envelopes came through our letterbox – one with £500 in cash, the other with £1,000. God is good! This was the miraculous gift of generous giving in action.

When we look around, there are many people operating in this gift, and the exciting news is there are no limitations on who can participate. What is generous to one person could be loose change to another, but for the recipient it is the sign of a miracle and tangible proof of God's love. Moving in this gift is incredibly personal; only you and God know if you are truly being generous.

It shouldn't surprise us that God, whose generosity has no limits, has ensured operating in this gift is good for us. Researchers from the Department of Psychology at the University of Lübeck in Germany conducted an experiment with fifty volunteers on how generosity impacts the human brain. To summarise a complex piece of research, while they knew that generosity was common and a more spontaneous behaviour than greed, they also discovered that those who made the most generous decisions were also the happiest. This was despite the personal cost to themselves.[31] Great news: being generous makes us happy! It is part of God's crazy upside-down kingdom that we gain by giving.

As Proverbs 11:24-25 says:

The world of the generous gets larger and larger;
the world of the stingy gets smaller and smaller.
The one who blesses others is abundantly blessed;
those who help others are helped.
(The Message)

Adam Grant, Wharton's top-rated professor, suggests that people fit into one of three reciprocity styles that he calls Givers, Takers and Matchers. He expands upon this by declaring: 'Whereas takers strive to get as much as

---

[31] www.trustbridgeglobal.com/blog/2019/9/13/generosity-and-happiness? (accessed 18th August 2023).

possible from others and matchers aim to trade evenly, givers are the rare breed of people who contribute to others without expecting anything in return.'[32]

Despite our nature, we should always aim to be generous givers, irrespective of whether this is our spiritual gift.

On a recent holiday, we embarked on a trip to a local beach for an evening of traditional entertainment and food. Before the evening properly began, and upon reaching our destination, we strolled along the beach and came across a British couple and a local lad. The couple had been fishing all day and the boy, who was deaf and unable to speak, had been helping them. Owing to his disabilities, he was unable to attend school, and lacked even basic education. There was no dad on the scene and Mum worked in the local shop. In an already impoverished island, his future didn't look promising.

We spent about thirty minutes with this happy little trio until the couple started to pack away their fishing rods, reels, etc and prepared to return to their hotel. Before they left, they handed over most of their fishing paraphernalia, totalling in excess of £1,000, to the local boy as an investment in his future. The couple confided they'd need to save to replace what they had given away, but as fishing could provide an income for this boy who had served them all day, and the potential of a brighter future, it was worth it. We all went our separate ways feeling happier and with big smiles.

---

[32] https://adamgrant.net/book/give-and-take (accessed 18th August 2023).

In our survey 57.1 per cent believed that the more you practise generosity, the easier it becomes.

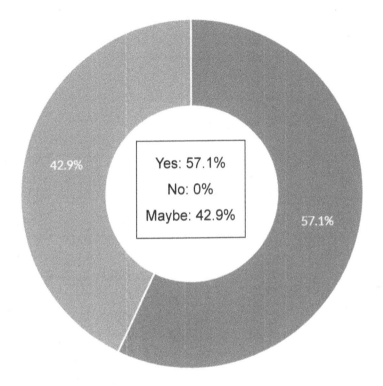

I would guess that for this openhanded couple it wasn't the first and it won't be the last time that they move in the gift of generous giving.

American author Kent Nerburn shares:

Giving is a miracle that can transform the heaviest of hearts. Two people, who moments before lived in separate worlds of private concerns, suddenly meet each other over a simple act of sharing. The world expands, a moment of goodness is created, and

something new comes into being where before there
was nothing.[33]

Most of the time when we move in the gift of generous giving, it is not because we have an abundance of finances or because we want to feel good about ourselves. It is because we have been moved by the Holy Spirit and we want to share our faith, what we have, with the world.

We see this in the account of Mary pouring expensive perfume onto Jesus' feet, wiping them with her hair and filling the room with scent as an act of love and worship in John 12:3. This was extravagance on a grand scale! It was also obedience and set an example that others should follow. In the background of the Gospels are Mary, Joanna and Susanna who generously financially support Jesus and the disciples.[34] Many missionaries, church leaders and Christian charities would not exist without the support of a faithful few.

In one of the charities I worked with, there was an individual who not only funded several costly projects that greatly impacted families within the UK and brought many to faith, but they also left a sizable legacy in their will. This is abundant generosity!

In 2 Corinthians 4, the apostle Paul talks honestly about his struggles and encourages us to 'fix our eyes not on what is seen, but on what is unseen, since what is seen is temporary, but what is unseen is eternal' (verse 18).

So much of our focus tends to be on the immediate, on the things that can be touched and seen. I want to suggest

---

[33] www.kentnerburn.com/thoughts-on-giving (accessed 18th August 2023).
[34] Luke 8:1-3.

that when we give generously, when we are obedient to the Holy Spirit and move in this gifting, we are leaving a spiritual legacy, investing in another and looking beyond the horizon to eternity.

I believe with all my heart that generosity breeds generosity. This is because generosity is extremely contagious, and when we give generously, the ripple effect will continue to create more generosity in the world. A good friend, Lesley Whipps, shared this story with me:

Every year our church offers free Christmas gift wrapping to the people Christmas shopping in the city. We buy good quality wrapping paper, ribbons, bows and tags. We wrap as many presents as the people need all free of charge, not even taking donations. If people insist on giving money, we ask them to donate to a charity of their choice. Once people get their head around the fact that it's all free it can lead on to some great conversations! On one occasion a man insisted we take a £10 donation for our generosity. Within minutes some grandparents asked us to wrap some gifts for their grandchildren. A conversation was had and it turned out that the grandchildren's home had burned down, resulting in the family losing everything. The £10 donation was immediately given to the grandparents so they could buy something extra for the grandchildren. A little later the grandparents returned again with some books they had bought for the grandchildren. They asked that before they were wrapped someone would write on the inside cover, 'With love from the Elim church'. I don't know who was more blessed that day, the original recipient who made the donation, the grandparents, the grandchildren or the Elim church! I think it was everyone!

Generosity breeds generosity; it is contagious, and I pray we all catch it. Can you imagine how different our churches would be, how different the world would be? Dream with me of a time when your church leader or CEO stands at the front of the church or at your annual AGM and says, as Moses declared in Exodus 36:6, and I paraphrase, 'No more offerings, we have more than we need, the people have given enough.'[35] Can you imagine how disappointed and frustrated those who had delayed their gifts must have felt? God's work was finished, but they had excluded themselves from any share in it.

We cannot share personal stories of generosity if we are not creating them first. In Matthew 5:14-16 Jesus describes the disciples as 'the light of the world' and encourages us to 'let your light shine before others, that they may see your good deeds and glorify your Father in heaven'. It is incredibly powerful when people share stories of giving generously as it inspires others by providing a glimpse into another way to live and another way to serve God. The end goal of our generosity should always be for other people to see the glory, majesty and love of our heavenly Father. However, in the next chapter we are told:

---

[35] This is an exception, and I would suggest that unless it is clearly for the others' benefit, we should never take away the blessing that comes with giving.

Be careful not to practise your righteousness in front of others to be seen by them. If you do, you will have no reward from your Father in heaven.

So when you give to the needy, do not announce it with trumpets, as the hypocrites do in the synagogues and on the streets, to be honoured by others. Truly I tell you, they have received their reward in full. But when you give to the needy, do not let your left hand know what your right hand is doing, so that your giving may be in secret. Then your Father, who sees what is done in secret, will reward you.
(Matthew 6:1-4)

These verses hone in on motivation. Generous acts, done for God's sake and His glory, should be allowed to shine out and be seen as an encouragement to others and declaration of how great God is. We see this several times in Scripture, including in Acts 4:32-37 where we are told that 'from time to time' believers would sell land or houses and openly gift the proceeds to the apostles to be distributed as needed. However, if your motivation and desire is for you to be seen, then I'd suggest you keep your giving between you and God. We are all on a journey to become more like Jesus, and whether we are ready to hand the glory to God now or at some point in the future, this should not act as a barrier to you moving in financial generosity but should guide your steps in whether you share this act with others.

When we commit to glorifying God through our stories of generous giving, it becomes contagious.

To finish this chapter and to encourage you, here are some testimonies and comments about generosity shared by those who took part in the survey. My prayer is that you will be encouraged by what you read and inspired to move greatly and generously.

I have heard many, many remarkable stories but the most amazing thing to me is that any church of any size is able to function and thrive on the pure generosity and faith of its attendees.

Passing on a car to someone who needed it when the previous owner no longer needed it. Has happened quite a lot in our church and we've had/done both.

In 2018, as a church we spoke on financial generosity and wanted to teach the church practically on this. We announced an offering and that we would give the entirety of it away. We raised nearly 40K and were able to bless three local charities in the town.

When we worked in London we knew an elderly lady … who had a dreadful life story, having been sold into sex slavery as a child by her father to fund his gambling debts. Somehow, she had survived and lived on a basic state pension in a miserable little … flat. Yet she had a jar on the mantelpiece where she put any loose change she had. She used it to buy cake ingredients. When anyone in our community was having a tough time, she would appear on the doorstep with a cake just to tell us we were loved and that she was praying for us. She had nothing, really, but from what she had she gave something that impacted a whole community.

I've felt led to give a big chunk of my 'pension' away in obedience to Holy Spirit. Didn't see that one coming!

When I worked for a Christian youth charity, I had a team of supporters who funded at least 50 per cent of my salary – sometimes up to 80 per cent. It was amazing.

Questions

- Have you ever given any thought to generous giving being a gift of the Spirit?

- Like the story shared about the boy and the fishing equipment, what examples of generous giving have impacted you?

- More than half of those surveyed said they believe the more you practise generosity the easier it becomes. Do you agree with this? Why/Why not?

- Can you envisage a time when you would share about your own acts of generosity to encourage others? If anything, what would hold you back?

- Do you recognise the gift of generous giving in yourself? Is there someone you could confide in who could help you develop and grow in this gifting?

5

Thrown Like Confetti

Recently I bumped in to an ex-work colleague at an event she didn't know I was attending, *but* she had brought a cup to give me that I had admired on her social media page. Was she crazy to bring a cup for an individual who had no logical reason to be at the event? No, she was being obedient. She had no way of knowing I had been invited along, but she did know that God had prompted her to buy me that cup and to take it to that event. The logo on the cup read, 'Throw kindness around like confetti'. I love that!

I wholeheartedly embrace the concept of kindness being thrown around like confetti, as I appreciate being on the receiving end of kindness. It costs nothing to be kind to another person, but it can change everything. Kindness often expresses itself as being helpful and caring about other people.

Kindness is a fruit of the Spirit,[36] and giving generously we know is a gift, but I want to suggest the two go hand in hand. I loved the cup I was given because of the kind, caring nature in which it was given. If it had been lobbed

---

[36] Galatians 5:22-23.

at me from across the room or more mildly pushed towards me with a grunt, I'm sure I wouldn't treasure it as much as I do.

In this chapter we are looking at the immense kindness and generosity of God. How, even if we were to try, every second of every minute of every day for the rest of our lives, it would be impossible to outgive God.

For followers of Jesus, this is important. Jesus represents the Father and He is generous, which means as part of our journey of discipleship, where He becomes more and we become less, we need to become more generous too.

We need to be people of generosity

A couple of years ago, I shared most of the contents of this book with the church I co-pastor. While prepping, I realised that neither I nor my husband had ever preached on this subject before, and I felt awful. It was totally remiss of us and, if I'm being honest, I felt that as individuals and as a church we may have missed out. I know this sounds dramatic, but the reason for my regret will become clearer.

We all know that God is the greatest giver of all; no one can outgive God. John 3:16 tells us that 'God so loved the world that he *gave* his one and only Son' (emphasis mine). One of the many ways God expresses His love is by giving. God is the ultimate giver.

Did you know, it is possible to give without loving, but it is impossible to love and not give? I love to give gifts. I'm not always a great gift giver, but there's something so special about giving a gift to someone and seeing the smile on their face.

We have just celebrated our eldest son's thirtieth birthday. We enjoyed decorating his home with banners, sprinkling the table that we dined at with shiny sprinkles and presenting him with his own nostalgic party bag. There was great delight in seeing his eyes light up at each gift and surprise. These gifts were an extension, a tangible expression, of our love for him.

If we turn to Scripture, I believe all we can ever learn about giving being a tangible expression of love, we learn from God. In every book of the Bible, we read how He gave of Himself. The hints that we read in the Old Testament come to fruition in the New Testament when He gave His Son, who then gave His life that we might live. But it doesn't end there – while preparing His disciples for His departure, Jesus told them that God would 'give you another advocate to help you and be with you for ever— the Spirit of truth' (John 14:16-17). Our God gives, and gives and gives.

So familiar

As Christians we can become so familiar with this truth that it stops impacting us. We can know it, believe it, but not feel it.

Right at the beginning in the book of Genesis we read that God gave – He created the heavens and the earth. The earth was empty but God filled it with creative generosity. We only have to observe the brilliance of a sunset, wander around a zoo or meander through the countryside to see that this world God created is overflowing with elaborate detail and inconceivable harmony. There is so much variety everywhere we look, and it is captivating. This is

74

regularly evidenced by programmes such as *Blue Planet* and *Planet Earth*, that focus on God's creation and regularly attract millions of viewers[37] across a wide range of ages.[38] We are fascinated by what God has gifted us.

We know so much about the earth, but there are large areas that are still unknown to us, which means there are more thrilling discoveries to be made. Despite many of us paddling in the sea, we know more about the moon and Mars than we do of our own ocean floor. We know the ocean covers about 71 per cent of the earth's surface, but less than 20 per cent has ever been mapped. What we do know is mind-blowing, as below the waves oceanographers have discovered 'towering mountain ranges and deep canyons'. Two of these canyons are so deep that if Mount Everest, the world's tallest mountain and measuring more than five miles high, were placed there, its peak would not break the ocean's surface.[39] I wonder if we'll ever explore the remaining 80 per cent and what we'll find when we do! I often imagine God anticipating our delight when we uncover new things.

If we move our gaze upwards, the stars in the sky are an awesome example of God's generosity. We live in the Oxfordshire countryside and I love seeing the stars. Stars exist in vast groups called galaxies. The Milky Way is one such galaxy, containing the sun and approximately a hundred thousand million stars. In addition to the Milky

---

[37] www.theguardian.com/media/2017/nov/06/blue-planet-ii-years-most-watched-tv-show-david-attenborough (accessed 21st July 2023).

[38] www.sciencealert.com/more-young-people-are-watching-david-attenborough-than-the-x-factor (accessed 24th July 2023).

[39] education.nationalgeographic.org/resource/ocean (accessed 28th July 2023).

Way, there are millions upon millions of other galaxies which means countless trillions of stars.[40] In a throwaway line in Genesis 1:16 we are told God 'also made the stars'. A friend recently braved wild camping in Dartmoor for her granddaughter's birthday and described the sky as not having enough room for the millions of stars it needed to contain.

That is our abundantly generous God.

Never-ending generosity

So much thought went into the world we often take for granted.

In Genesis 1:26 we read:

> Then God said, 'Let us make mankind in our image, in our likeness, so that they may rule over the fish in the sea and the birds in the sky, over the livestock and all the wild animals, and over all the creatures that move along the ground.'

In verse 29 this is extended to include 'every seed-bearing plant on the face of the whole earth and every tree that has fruit with seed in it'.

God not only created us; He also provides for us. We see this time and time again throughout Scripture and in our normal, everyday lives. I love testimony time at our church, as we get a glimpse of the Father who loves to give. I remember one man, who I'll call Steve, sharing how he was driving and asked for a sign that God was real, that

---

[40] www.esa.int/Science_Exploration/Space_Science/Herschel/How_many_stars_are_there_in_the_Universe (accessed 28th July 2023).

He heard his prayers. At the next set of traffic lights he stopped behind a van that had written in the grime of the van, 'I love you, Steve'. God is in the details.

Or another friend who lives in a sizeable home and whose husband had lost an item that he had searched high and low for. After he grumbled about this lost item, she responded by saying, 'I'll ask God where it is.' Upon receiving her answer, she went to the destination God had revealed and retrieved the 'lost' item. Like any good Father, He loves being part of our lives.

God's generosity doesn't end with gifting us life and everything on the earth, because He also enables us to reproduce. Even the act of lovemaking is a gift, and for couples, an opportunity to express affection, honour and respect.

This is our God! He is good, generous, thorough and never short-sighted. He knows and understands our needs before we even realise there is a need.

In addition to this, His generosity is never-ending; it is seen year in and year out. Psalm 65:9-13 tells us:

> You care for the land and water it;
> you enrich it abundantly.
> The streams of God are filled with water
> to provide the people with corn,
> for so you have ordained it.
> You drench its furrows and level its ridges;
> you soften it with showers and bless its crops.
> You crown the year with your bounty,
> and your carts overflow with abundance.
> The grasslands of the wilderness overflow;
> the hills are clothed with gladness.

The meadows are covered with flocks
and the valleys are mantled with corn;
they shout for joy and sing.

And if that wasn't enough, God's giving overflows into blessing. In Malachi 3:10, a text we'll look at in more detail later, God promises:

'Bring the whole tithe into the storehouse, that there may be food in my house. Test me in this,' says the LORD Almighty, 'and see if I will not throw open the floodgates of heaven and pour out so much blessing that there will not be room enough to store it.'

It is part of God's nature to be generous and to give, and He wants us to be the same. In fact, this is part of our discipleship journey, this is part of us becoming more like Him. 1 John 4:19 says, 'We love because [God] first loved us.'

In the Sermon on the Mount, Jesus made this profusely and uncomfortably clear when He said:

And if anyone wants to sue you and take your shirt, hand over your coat as well. If anyone forces you to go one mile, go with them two miles. Give to the one who asks you, and do not turn away from the one who wants to borrow from you.
(Matthew 5:40-42)

How easy would it be for you to do this? Or maybe I should ask, how easy do you find *doing* this?

Recently my husband and I stumbled across the film *3:10 to Yuma*. The story focuses on a small-time rancher who agrees to hold a captured outlaw. One of the lawmen who captured the outlaw decides to take his horse. In an act of revenge, the outlaw grabs a knife and kills the lawmen. His reason for this was, 'He took my horse,' and elaborated by stating, 'It's man's nature to take what we want. That's how we're born.'

As people made in the 'image of God' (Genesis 1:27), we may be uncomfortable with the idea that to take is part of our nature as it sounds so cynical and very unChristian. But I want to suggest it's in God's nature to give, and to give generously, and it's inherent in our fallen nature to take. However, this isn't black and white, there are – like life in general – grey areas.

If we go back to Genesis and some of the scriptures we've already touched on, God gives and gives. His generosity is staggering and still being appreciated by us today as He is the Father who gives 'good gifts' (Matthew 7:11). Then in Genesis 3, we see the first take. Eve, watched and then followed by Adam, takes the forbidden fruit from the tree of the knowledge of good and evil.

We know this was a game-changer, a moment that impacted the world, as it was at this point that sin entered in to the human heart, and humanity, made in the image of a generous and giving God, became takers. If you think about all the various wars that have occurred, in the main they have begun because people wanted to own more. They wanted to take what wasn't theirs.

If we look at those who have been convicted of a crime, of the 97,700 people currently in a UK prison, approximately 20 per cent are there after being found guilty of trying to obtain something that was not legally theirs.[41] This figure doesn't take into account those who took something that wasn't morally theirs.

To take is part of our nature, and when we look through the Old Testament, our family history, it is full of takers.

In Genesis 4, Cain sees that God approves of Abel's offering but not his, so he takes his brother's life and commits the first murder in history.

Further into Genesis, we read that Jacob is born grasping his brother's heel, takes his brother's birthright and tricks him out of his father's blessing.

In 2 Samuel 11, King David took Bathsheba then took the life of Uriah, her husband, even though in 1 Samuel 13:14 David is described as a man after the Lord's heart.

King Ahab wanted Naboth's vineyard. Naboth wouldn't sell; Ahab sulked and his wife, Jezebel, arranged for Naboth to be slaughtered so possession of the vineyard could be theirs. Read the story in 1 Kings 21.

The list goes on. But that's not the end of the story; we are all on a journey – as we become less so He becomes more. Our base instinct to take and accumulate can be overcome.

If we look at the end of Acts 7 and the story of Saul, we see him standing as one of the witnesses as Stephen is stoned to death. And later, Acts 9:1-2 tells us:

> Meanwhile, Saul was still breathing out murderous threats against the Lord's disciples. He went to the high priest and asked him for letters to the synagogues in Damascus, so that if he found any

[41] researchbriefings.files.parliament.uk/documents/SN04334/SN04334. pdf (accessed 16th July 2024).

there who belonged to the Way, whether men or women, he might take them as prisoners to Jerusalem.

We know that he then went on to have a powerful encounter with Jesus, was changed radically and was renamed Paul. He moved from persecuting Christians to being shipwrecked, imprisoned and beaten in the pursuit of sharing the gospel.[42]

Matthew, we know, had a similar conversion in that we are first introduced to him while he is a despised tax collector. After meeting with Jesus, he leaves behind a life of wealth and security for poverty and uncertainty.[43] He abandons the pleasures of this world for the promise of eternal life.

The story of humanity is littered with accounts of people meeting with Jesus and undertaking a lifelong mission of becoming more like Him. When we meet with Jesus we see God.[44]

And our God is amazingly, mind-blowingly generous. He has modelled what we can mimic. Just like we learned from those older and wiser when we were children, we can do the same in our growth with God. He has shown us how to live a life of abundant generosity. Everything is there for us; we need to decide if this is a lesson we want to learn and a lifestyle we want to adopt.

---

[42] Read his story in the book of Acts.

[43] Matthew 9:9.

[44] John 14:8-9.

Questions

- Have you ever been miraculously used to bless someone, or been blessed, like my friend blessed me with the cup?

- Do you agree that kindness and generosity go hand in hand? Are there any other 'fruits' that you would add?

- We know we cannot outgive God. What aspects of God's amazing generosity do you most appreciate, and why?

- How do you feel about the statement 'it's in God's nature to give, and to give generously, and it's inherent in our nature to take'? Can you provide an explanation for your feelings?

- Do you agree that within our own limitations we can mimic God's amazing generosity? Why/why not?

6
Let's Talk About Tithing...

I know this may be controversial, but in my opinion, you can't have a book on generosity without looking at tithing. I'm aware some of you may have tithed for years, while some are not even sure if it's still relevant or expected.

My reason for including this chapter isn't to annoy you, evoke feelings of guilt or teach you theology you know inside out, but simply because tithing involves money, centres on generosity and therefore, for the subject we are looking at, is essential.

In the survey we distributed, 79.3 per cent believed it still to be a key part of our discipleship journey, while 20.7 per cent were unsure.

My prayers are that this chapter will affirm the 79.3 per cent and help answer some of the questions for the 20.7 per cent. To help do this, we will look at the theology behind tithing in this chapter and then how applicable it is for us today in the next chapter.

When we read the Old Testament, we need to remove our modern glasses. Our twenty-first-century perspective means our worldview, shaped by the culture we live in, tends to assess behavioural matters in terms of their

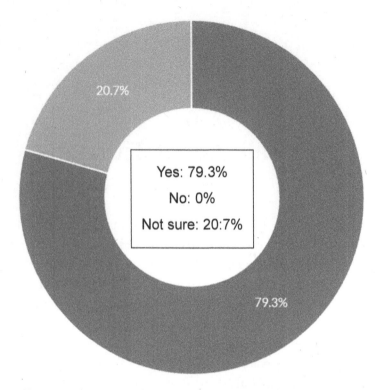

Yes: 79.3%
No: 0%
Not sure: 20:7%

20.7%

79.3%

effects on the individual, whereas the Old Testament is the story of a communal experience, with the concern and framework focused on the integrity and wholeness of the community.[45] With this in mind, let's delve into the Old Testament.

We first see tithing when Abraham gave one-tenth of the spoils of war to Melchizedek, the priest-king of Salem:

> Then Melchizedek king of Salem brought out bread and wine. He was priest of God Most High, and he blessed Abram, saying,

---

[45] Thomas H Jeavons and Rebekah Burch Basinger, *Growing Givers Hearts* (Hoboken, NJ: Jossey-Bass, 2007), p 40.

'Blessed be Abram by God Most High,
Creator of heaven and earth.
And praise be to God Most High,
who delivered your enemies into your hand.'
Then Abram gave him a tenth of everything.
(Genesis 14:18-20)

This is a fantastic example of mutual blessing, with the bigger picture being that Melchizedek is seen to be a 'type' of Christ.[46]

The next spontaneous tithe appears in Genesis 28:20-22:

Then Jacob made a vow, saying, 'If God will be with me and will watch over me on this journey I am taking and will give me food to eat and clothes to wear so that I return safely to my father's household, then the LORD will be my God and this stone that I have set up as a pillar will be God's house, and of all that you give me I will give you a tenth.'

Just like his grandfather Abraham, Jacob chose to worship God financially. The Hebrew word for 'tithe' translates to 'tenth', and when we tithe to God, we are giving back 10 per cent of our income to Him.

Introduction to tithing

In Deuteronomy 14:22-27 we are given more guidance and regulation around tithing, which we are going to walk through verse by verse:

---

[46] See Hebrews 7.

> Be sure to set aside a tenth of all that your fields produce each year. (v22)

Here we have the confirmation that we are expected to give back 10 per cent. For many people, the mention of 10 per cent is enough to put them off tithing. To tithe takes away a lot of what we have; 2 per cent is manageable, at 5 per cent we'd feel the pinch, but 10 per cent is a sacrifice.

And that's the point: it's meant to be a sacrifice. Abraham in Genesis 14 and Jacob in Genesis 28, the first two to tithe in the Bible, gave willingly in response to God's blessing and provision – their tithes were given as a sacrifice and in worship.

In Genesis 26:5, God says, 'Abraham obeyed me and did everything I required of him, keeping my commands, my decrees and my instructions.' This language mirrors later instructions regarding the Mosaic Law and implies that laws in addition to those written in Genesis were given to God's people.

The late, great William Barclay expanded upon this by stating:

> It's clear from Genesis 4 that the first family knew they had a responsibility to give back to God a portion of what God had given them. They were even held responsible for the kind of offering they gave. God accepted Abel's offering and rejected Cain's. In addition, since the Old Testament later links the offering of the 'firstborn' and 'firstfruits' to the tithe, it's possible Abel's offering was accepted precisely because it was a tithe. The Old Testament is clear God's people were to give back to him—and

that he'd given instructions about what that entailed.[47]

When we give to God, when we tithe, this forms a part of our worship to Him. With our worship, we are saying that God has worth, that He is worthy. Worship means to declare worth, to attribute worth.

King David, in 2 Samuel 24, needs to seek repentance as he has sinned, which results in God sending a plague, and he goes to the threshing floor of Araunah to offer up a sacrifice and build an altar. David is told there is no charge for him to do this, he can take whatever oxen and materials he wants. But he insists on paying and replies, 'I will not sacrifice to the LORD my God burnt offerings that cost me nothing' (v24).

To worship God is to give Him His worth. I want to suggest that the only giving that counts as acceptable worship has an element of sacrifice. Back to Deuteronomy 14:

> Eat the tithe of your corn, new wine and olive oil, and the firstborn of your herds and flocks in the presence of the LORD your God at the place he will choose as a dwelling for his Name, so that you may learn to revere the LORD your God always. (v23)

In the days when worship involved feasting, tithing became an essential part of communal worship. In fact, without the tithe, such worship would have been impossible. These days, without tithes it would be

---

[47] www.thegospelcoalition.org/article/bible-commands-christians-to-tithe/ (accessed 28th August 2023).

impossible for many churches to own or use a building or employ a minister.

Take a second to let that soak in – through our tithes, our honouring of God, we make that possible.

When we look at the text, we are called to bring the firstborn, which was typically the biggest and the best. As most of us are not active farmers, it can be confusing to see how the 'firstborn' relates to us. I want to suggest it means we not only give 10 per cent but we also give the first 10 per cent.

If we wonder whether God will really mind if we hold back, we only need to look at Malachi 3:8-10:

> 'Will a mere mortal rob God? Yet you rob me.
>   'But you ask, "How are we robbing you?"
>   'In tithes and offerings. You are under a curse – your whole nation – because you are robbing me. Bring the whole tithe into the storehouse, that there may be food in my house. Test me in this,' says the LORD Almighty, 'and see if I will not throw open the floodgates of heaven and pour out so much blessing that there will not be room enough to store it.'

God does not sugarcoat it or soften His words when He declares keeping back part of our tithe, not giving the full 10 per cent, is effectively robbing Him.

We are told to bring the tithe into the storehouse so 'there may be food in my house'. His house is His church and His church is His people. I believe in this bit of Scripture we are being told, really clearly, that our tithe should go to the church we attend, not to a missionary, not to an amazing charity (and there are many), but to God's house. This is my interpretation, as the church you attend is God's collective, detectable and visible presence in your community.

Then, in an almost unprecedented fashion, God challenges His people to test Him when He says 'the floodgates of heaven' will be thrown open and He will 'pour out so much blessing that there will not be room enough to store it'. Tithing is always a test of faith. It's big enough to hurt and forces us to trust God to provide. God asks us to test Him in this and God's blessings come in all shapes and forms.

But why would God, who has heavenly storehouses and the riches of the world at His fingertips, care if someone held back some of their tithe? Although God asks for 10 per cent, this could be 10 per cent of £100 or 10 per cent of £1 million; in that sense it's never about the amount, but God cares because what we give says so much about our attitude towards Him.

Giving to God helps us grow closer to God; it has an impact on our faith life, which helps us to see God's blessings in the everyday. For the Israelites, giving 10 per cent was as much a sacrifice for them as it can be for us, but as they responded in obedience, God responded in blessing. Deuteronomy 28:2-6 tells us:

> All these blessings will come on you and accompany you if you obey the LORD your God:
>
> You will be blessed in the city and blessed in the country.
>
> The fruit of your womb will be blessed, and the crops of your land and the young of your livestock

– the calves of your herds and the lambs of your flocks.

Your basket and your kneading trough will be blessed.

You will be blessed when you come in and blessed when you go out.

This is not 'prosperity preaching'; we don't give to God to receive or to try to manipulate Him – we give because He gave first. We give because He is worthy. We give to be obedient. We give because He is such a generous God that we want to worship Him, and He responds to that attitude with blessings.

Our giving to God is similar to a Mother's Day experience I had many years ago when both our sons were fairly young. My husband was working and had forgotten to give our boys some money to buy me a card and present. They were desperate to buy me something and I was very happy to receive. In order for this to happen, we needed to visit the bank so I could withdraw money from my account which I then gifted to them so they could buy me a present. Even thought it was bought with my money, they loved presenting me with their gift and I loved receiving it. This is reminiscent of tithing in that we are simply and lovingly giving back to God what is already His.

For those of you who are finding this chapter a bit heavy, you'll like this next bit in Deuteronomy 14:

But if that place is too distant and you have been blessed by the LORD your God and cannot carry your tithe (because the place where the LORD will choose to put his Name is so far away), then exchange your tithe for silver, and take the silver with you and go to the place the LORD your God will choose. Use the silver to buy whatever you like: cattle, sheep, wine or other fermented drink, or anything you wish. Then you and your household shall eat there in the presence of the LORD your God and rejoice. (vv24-26)

What amazing flexibility! After emphasising the need to select the firstborn, God tells us, and I paraphrase, 'If you have too far to travel, don't worry about it. Sell your animals and crops and bring the equivalent in money.'

When you're ready to worship God with a feast, bring whatever you like, anything you wish – meat, salad, cakes, drinks – whatever you fancy, a bit like a typical bring and share lunch at church. As someone who really enjoys but doesn't know how to cook jollof rice, I love these lunches!

Although tithing is a command, it culminated in God's people coming into God's presence and having a party that was full of joy, brimming with worship, enjoying being with each other and with their Creator. It was a fun place to be. This is the result of tithing.

Remember 2 Corinthians 9:7, 'God loves a cheerful giver.' You know why God loves a cheerful giver? Because attitude is important, and no one likes a party pooper. The next verse of Deuteronomy 14 tells us:

And do not neglect the Levites living in your towns, for they have no land allotted to them or any inheritance of their own. (v27)

Tithing we know is a way of supporting the ministries that flow from the Church and those called into full-time ministry. Can you imagine the difference if *every* Christian were to tithe 10 per cent? That would be amazing. We could revolutionise the world we live in!

A study done by the National Churches Trust shows that in 2021 the economic and social value of church buildings to the UK, by way of services rendered, including food banks, supporting those in need within their communities through pay it forward schemes, volunteer opportunities that help people build self-esteem and maintain good mental health, etc, contributed £55 billion to the UK economy.[48] In addition, they found that for every £1 invested in a church, the return based on the services provided, is over £16.[49] This is an eye-watering, jaw-dropping amount.

Again, can you imagine the difference Christians in the UK could make in His name if every Christian were obedient and gave 10 per cent? We could do amazing things that would impact this land, help spread the gospel far and wide, proving an impossibility for others to ignore.

Why is the tithe important to God?

God, we know, is awesome, He is generous and mind-blowingly creative. Why would our heavenly Father want

[48] www.nationalchurchestrust.org/news/annual-social-value-uks-church-buildings-over-%25C2%25A355-billion (accessed 18th August 2023).

[49] www.nationalchurchtrust.org/sites/default/files/GADS1597%20%E2%80%93%20NCT%20House%20of%20Good%202021%20V7%20SINGLE-PAGES.pdf (accessed 16th July 2024).

to separate for Himself a portion of all that He provided and require that it be returned to Him?

I want to suggest it is because God knew the abundance and blessings He provides would compete for our affection and challenge our commitment to Him. Tithing is a tangible way for us to choose God over the things in this world.

When we tithe, we acknowledge where our provision comes from and we declare that all we have is from God; that He has faithfully provided for our needs and we are returning a portion to Him as a tangible expression of our submission, love and worship.

I believe the blessing of tithing is multifaceted. Sometimes the blessing occurs through our faith being strengthened, our dependency being deepened, ministry being provided for or those in need being cared for. At all times my belief and experience has been that it benefits the individual and the community.

Through the power of giving, God helps us to have hearts more like His, to be generous, to be people who want to give.

Questions

- In the survey, 79.3 per cent believed tithing to be a key part of our discipleship journey while 20.7 per cent were unsure. What do you believe, and why?

- Do you think the cultural differences between now and the Old Testament impact our worldview of tithing?

- Which of the scriptures we looked at (if any) offers a new or different perspective from that which you already held?

- We looked briefly at the importance of attitude regarding tithing and how it forms part of our worship to God. Is this something you can relate to? Do you see the tithe as a way of worshipping God?

- Were you surprised by the figures released in the study done by the National Churches Trust? What impact do you think the Church could have if everyone were to tithe?

7

How Do I Give in the Twenty-first Century?

Two men were marooned on an island. One man paced back and forth, worried and scared, while the other man sat back and was sunning himself. The first man said, 'Aren't you afraid we are about to die?'

'No,' said the second man. 'I make £10,000 a week and tithe faithfully to my church. My pastor will find me.'[50]

Throughout this chapter we will explore the relevance of tithing and giving in the twenty-first century against the backdrop that Christians in the UK give on average 2.5 per cent of their monthly income to Christian causes.[51]

However, as we move from the Old Testament to the New Testament, we have to adjust our lens. No longer are we focusing on the communal experience, but rather on an individual's relationship with God.

From this relationship, formed under New Covenant grace, there is an expectation that from the love and gratitude an individual has for God, generosity will flow.

---

[50] Source unknown.

[51] www.stewardship.org.uk/generosity-report (accessed 5th July 2024).

This can be summarised by the simple instructions Jesus gives to His disciples in Matthew 10:8 as He sends them out: 'Freely you have received; freely give.'

In order to look at whether tithing is still relevant today, I want us to look at the past and specifically Malachi 3:6-10:

> 'I the LORD do not change. So you, the descendants of Jacob, are not destroyed. Ever since the time of your ancestors you have turned away from my decrees and have not kept them. Return to me, and I will return to you,' says the LORD Almighty.
>
> 'But you ask, "How are we to return?"
>
> 'Will a mere mortal rob God? Yet you rob me.
>
> 'But you ask, "How are we robbing you?"
>
> 'In tithes and offerings. You are under a curse – your whole nation – because you are robbing me. Bring the whole tithe into the storehouse, that there may be food in my house. Test me in this,' says the LORD Almighty, 'and see if I will not throw open the floodgates of heaven and pour out so much blessing that there will not be room enough to store it.'

This is a portion of Scripture that we are all familiar with, have dipped into previously in this book and have probably read numerous times, but I want to highlight one really key point.

Malachi 3:6 starts with the declaration, 'I the LORD do not change.' If tithing, giving back to God, showing that we consider Him to be worthy of our worship, was important to God in the Old Testament, I want to suggest it is equally as important now, as while His practices may change, God's principles do not.

As John writes in his Gospel, Jesus is the very Word of God, made flesh.[52] Or, as the author of Hebrews says in Hebrews 1:1-2, the very speech of God. Every thread in the tapestry of the Law and Prophets converges on Him. And as the incarnate Word, He upholds every requirement of the Law as seen in Matthew 5:17-19, when Jesus states:

> Do not think that I have come to abolish the Law or the Prophets; I have not come to abolish them but to fulfil them. For truly I tell you, until heaven and earth disappear, not the smallest letter, not the least stroke of a pen, will by any means disappear from the Law until everything is accomplished. Therefore anyone who sets aside one of the least of these commands and teaches others accordingly will be called least in the kingdom of heaven, but whoever practises and teaches these commands will be called great in the kingdom of heaven.

Later on in Matthew 23:23, Jesus berates the Pharisees for their commitment to one part of God's law, the tithe, while neglecting 'the more important matters of the law – justice, mercy and faithfulness'. Then He declares, 'These you ought to have done, without neglecting the others' (ESV).

The Greek word translated 'ought' (*dei*) is strong, indicates a necessity and could be translated as follows: 'You must do these things, and you must not neglect those things.'[53]

---

[52] See John 1:1,14.

[53] www.thegospelcoalition.org/article/bible-commands-christians-to-tithe (accessed 28th August 2023).

We read at the very beginning of Matthew 23 that Jesus is teaching 'the crowds' and 'his disciples'. These words are for Jesus' followers, and in teaching His disciples, Jesus also teaches us the importance of tithing to God.

In my mind I can imagine Jesus, surrounded by His followers, sharing these truths and making sure all who are listening understand He's not discarding the promises, expectations and hopes of the prophets. He's not dismissing the holiness of God expressed in the Law of Moses. Rather, He is the fulfilment of all of those things.

Most of us would agree that observation of the Sabbath is still applicable today. Under the Mosaic Law, the Sabbath (an eternal law rooted in creation) had various restrictions which if broken could result in death.[54] Thankfully, under the New Covenant, the practices (restrictions) become unnecessary while the principle of the Sabbath remains.[55]

I believe the same is true of tithing; that bringing the tithe in to God's storehouse to support its work and mission is still relevant for Christians today. The legal requirement to tithe has been abolished but the principle, birthed by Abraham and Jacob, precedes the law and remains for the benefit of believers – the benefit being that tithing is a way to give your heart over to God because you're physically reminding yourself that He provides what you need and your security lies in Him alone.

---

[54] Numbers 15:32-36.
[55] Colossians 2:16.

Tough seasons

With the best intentions, tithing can be a challenge when life is going well, but what do we do when the tough seasons come along? Or when we really want to buy a new car or something extra special for our loved one's birthday? While there are some crisis situations where giving is an impossibility, such as losing your job, I suggest where possible it's good to be consistent with our tithe. If we do this over time, we begin to see the blessings that come from trusting God with our money, and learn to resist the fear of not having enough.

Unsurprisingly, when my husband and I stepped away from being financial advisers and became full-time Bible college students, our income was dramatically impacted. We both had part-time jobs at the college but were unable to give the full tithe and pay the bills. During this time, our income didn't cover our expenditure and we were reliant on the money from our recent house sale to survive. Despite this, we made the personal decision to give a percentage of what we earned back to God. I share this to encourage those who want to give to God, who want to worship Him in this way, but 10 per cent isn't possible during this season. If this is you and 10 per cent is too much, start by giving back to Him what you can afford, with the aim of increasing the amount when you are able to do so. Like we were, you might be surprised by how God blesses your obedience.

Over the years, I have had numerous people tell me they pay their tithe through serving and giving their time. These have been good, honest people who love Jesus but have got a bit confused. And I can understand why they have got confused, as tithing and serving are both ways to give, but each has a unique purpose. Tithing is a way to show that we prioritise God over money, whereas serving is a way of worshipping God through dedicating our time and talents to bless others and glorify His kingdom. Both are means of lavish generosity, are great ways to honour God and show love to others. But I believe the giving of our time via serving should be done in addition to our tithe, not as a replacement for it.

Living under New Covenant grace affords a certain amount of freedom. But I can testify that being outrageously generous with both money and time is great fun and potentially one of the best things we will ever do!

What do we mean by New Covenant grace?

In Malachi we find a clear notification that God wants us to engage our hearts and to be generous, like Him; that His desire is for us to use the freedom we have been given and to be children who not only give Him back 10 per cent of the 100 per cent He has gifted, but go beyond that and give an offering. When we understand that God owns it all, everything in our bank account, everything in our wallets, it becomes easier to give when He asks for it.

Conversely, easier doesn't mean the cost is less. As a Christian and someone who believes wholeheartedly in the principle of the tithe, I understand the cost. For example, there have been times when we have needed to cut down on car trips to delay the necessity to top up on fuel, or towards the end of the month we have prayerfully raided the freezer in search of that night's dinner. This would not have been needed if we didn't joyfully choose to financially give back to God.

There is an established grant-making trust that has impacted and aided the reach of the gospel and was initially founded by a godly and generous man called Sir John Laing CBE (1879-1978). Sir John Laing was a husband, father, British entrepreneur, philanthropist and Christian. In the book about his life there is a copy of his financial plan, and it reads as follows:

> If income is £400 per annum, give £50, live on £150, save £200.
>
> If income £1,000 per annum, give £200, live on £300 and save £500.
>
> If income £3000 per annum, give £1,000, live on £500, save £1,500.
>
> If income £4,000 per annum, give £1,500, live on £500, save £2,000.[56]

I share this partly because I find it inspiring, but also because while the level of giving increases from 12.5 to 37.5 per cent, his living expenditure does not rise above £500. Here we see the heart of Sir John Laing, his love for Jesus and willingness to worship Him with everything he has.[57] What a great example of moving in New Covenant grace and freedom.

---

[56] Alex McIlhinney, *The Service of Giving* (Scotland: OPAL Trust, 2022), p 8.

[57] McIlhinney, *The Service of Giving*, p 298. The abundant generosity and willing sacrifice of Sir John Laing is still felt today through the

The scripture we looked at earlier, Matthew 5:17, 'Do not think that I have come to abolish the Law or the Prophets; I have not come to abolish them but to fulfil them', continues in verse 20: 'For I say to you, that unless your righteousness exceeds *the righteousness* of the scribes and Pharisees, you will by no means enter the kingdom of heaven' (NKJV).

I believe this scripture is encouraging us to enlarge our hearts. And I believe this because when Jesus points to an Old Covenant law by saying he hadn't 'come to abolish' but to 'fulfil', and sets out an expectation that our righteousness should surpass the very legalistic Pharisees, He is teaching us an amazing lesson. He is spotlighting a higher standard. He is showing us ways we can spiritually grow and become mature.

The law said not to commit murder, but in Matthew 5:22, Jesus said to not be angry with a brother or sister. The law said not to commit adultery, but in Matthew 5:28, Jesus said don't even look at someone lustfully.

This is a higher standard. Sir John Laing's budget showed generosity of a higher standard.

This reminds me of the story I heard about the minister's child who, having drifted away from God, attended a Christian Union meeting, found his faith and started attending church. At one Sunday meeting he heard a sermon on tithing and was convicted. He was convicted to such an extent that he ran home, rang his minister dad

---

many grants that are annually gifted, with an estimated total from 1923 to 2021 being, in today's value, £76,704,501. This is an awesome amount and a great legacy from someone who knew the benefit of giving back to God and His people.

and said, 'Dad, I've just heard the most amazing sermon that will change your life. You won't believe the blessings and foundations of giving 10 per cent of your income to God – it's called tithing. I'm going to tithe and I think you should too.'

After a few seconds' silence, the dad replied, 'OK, son, you know best. I'll stop giving 20 per cent of my income and start giving 10 per cent.'

I don't know if this is a true story, and if it is, I don't really believe that the dad stopped giving 20 per cent, but as we have seen, being generous, giving to God is part of our discipleship journey, and clearly the dad was further along this journey than the son.

The minimum

New Covenant grace means we start with tithing as this is the minimum we should be giving back to God.

Then, as our hearts grow bigger, as we become more and more like Jesus, as we grow in godly generosity, we give more than 10 per cent.

Our 10 per cent, the first fruit, remains in God's house, the church that we know is His people, but when we look at offering, giving according to grace, we adhere to a higher standard. We do this because we love God, we acknowledge the money is His and we want to glorify, magnify and worship Him in every way possible.

Through my time as a fundraiser, I have seen ordinary people do extraordinary things that have made the impossible possible. This has happened through Christians giving offerings, and these sterling soldiers have marched into areas of need to share God's Word, truths, grace, hope and love.

The way we approach and distribute money says so much about who we are and where our priorities lie. Billy Graham once said, 'If people get their attitudes right towards money, it will help straighten out almost every other area of life.'[58]

We see this in the parable about the rich fool in Luke 12, who stored up things for himself, was stingy with God and then lost his life, or the story of the rich young ruler in Mark 10 who put money before God.

But perhaps the most graphic story and encouragement to live a life of generosity, of having a right attitude towards money, is found in Luke 16:19-29:

> There was a rich man who was dressed in purple and fine linen and lived in luxury every day. At his gate was laid a beggar named Lazarus, covered with sores and longing to eat what fell from the rich man's table. Even the dogs came and licked his sores.
>
> The time came when the beggar died and the angels carried him to Abraham's side. The rich man also died and was buried. In Hades, where he was in torment, he looked up and saw Abraham far away, with Lazarus by his side. So he called to him, 'Father Abraham, have pity on me and send Lazarus to dip the tip of his finger in water and cool my tongue, because I am in agony in this fire.'

[58] billygraham.org/answer/is-money-gods-outward-blessing-on-a-persons-life (28th August 2023).

But Abraham replied, 'Son, remember that in your lifetime you received your good things, while Lazarus received bad things, but now he is comforted here and you are in agony. And besides all this, between us and you a great chasm has been set in place, so that those who want to go from here to you cannot, nor can anyone cross over from there to us.'

He answered, 'Then I beg you, father, send Lazarus to my family, for I have five brothers. Let him warn them, so that they will not also come to this place of torment.'

Abraham replied, 'They have Moses and the Prophets; let them listen to them.'

We see that the rich man knew of Lazarus, but we don't read that he was actively nasty to him; he just had a complete disregard and lack of gracious generosity. I'm sure he wasn't being malicious; he had just stopped seeing Lazarus and probably all the other beggars. This is something we can all be guilty of.

When I worked full-time in central London, I stopped seeing the large number of homeless people. My heart no longer broke at their plight. It took seeing them through the eyes of my young daughter for the curtain of familiarity to be raised and for their plight to touch my heart. It can be the same when we see displaced people on the news or hear of a violent event. Our familiarity with these occurrences can cause our hearts to harden and stop us seeing the people behind the situations. We are unable to impact every life, but through gifts, offerings and operating in New Covenant grace, we can be loving and generous to the ones we are aware of.

The rich man had a daily opportunity to extend the love of Jesus to Lazarus, and throughout our lifetime we will have numerous opportunities to impact others.

Philippians 2:3-6 declares:

> Do nothing out of selfish ambition or vain conceit. Rather, in humility value others above yourselves, not looking to your own interests but each of you to the interests of the others.
> In your relationships with one another, have the same mindset as Christ Jesus:
> who, being in very nature God,
> did not consider equality with God something to be used to his own advantage.

Jesus lived a radical life; His teaching on giving was radical and requires a radical change of heart. You might be reading this and thinking, 'I'm not really a radical person. I'm more of a moderate personality.' If that's you, please relax and know that's fine because the change Jesus is looking for is internal.

Romans 5:5 tells us, 'And hope does not put us to shame, because God's love has been poured out into our hearts through the Holy Spirit, who has been given to us.' This love will show itself externally in a way that suits your God-given personality and the situation you find yourself in.

Many years ago, we used to buy clothes for a teenage girl we knew, but a 'middle man' handed them on. At the time we didn't want the parents of the teenage girl to feel a need to thank us, and we were more comfortable remaining anonymous. I don't think God minded that this was our preference. I hope He was pleased that we were showing love to one of His children and that we had the right attitude. There have been occasions when we have been happy for people to know that the gift has been from us, and times when we have directly placed the gift into the hands of the recipient. Different gifts and unique individuals have led to a variation of interactions.

Every week, from Monday to Friday, I am in contact with many people whose amazing financial generosity, which exceeds their tithe, shapes the nations – that's pretty radical. That's godly generosity. At the weekend I spend time as an ordained minister with a group of Christians, who through godly generosity are slowly but surely claiming their community for Jesus. Could both groups do more? Probably, but that's between them and God.

What's important is that we start to move in the right direction.

More generous life

Carolyn Davidson was a graphic design student at Portland State University. In 1969, she met Phil Knight, who knew Carolyn was in search of extra funds to take oil painting classes, so he asked her to help him out on some projects at a rate of $2 an hour.

Carolyn needed to come up with a logo, which she did, although by her own admission she wasn't pleased with what she'd designed and didn't think it was her best work. Phil, who'd commissioned the logo, apparently thought it was OK, but he didn't love it. Still, he used it and paid $35 for the design.

Today this simple tick, often described as the swoosh, is arguably one of the most iconic and recognisable logos of all time.

Because Carolyn didn't think this was her best work, I'm pretty sure she didn't go home floating on a cloud; it was just another day for her, nothing special, nothing out of the usual. She wasn't to know the impact of that day; she wasn't to know that on this ordinary day she did some of her best work.

I share this because there are things that you are doing now, from a radical heart, a heart bursting with love, faith, generosity and obedience that you may never know the impact of until you get to heaven.

There are also things that you should be doing that you've chosen not to, and I'd recommend you bring this before God.

God's plans for you are to prosper you. He wants you to live a generous life, a life that He can favour, a life that worships Him and shows His worth through tithing, blessing others and moving closer to Him.

When we give generously to others, we can know God's amazing river of grace. His abundance will never run out, and as we give to others, He will continue to give to us. When we give as declared in Malachi 3 (tithes and offerings), we will receive God's blessings.

In Luke 6:38, Jesus tells us the amount of blessing we receive will be in relation to the amount we give: 'Give, and it will be given to you. A good measure, pressed down, shaken together and running over, will be poured into your lap. For with the measure you use, it will be measured to you.'

Paul reinforces this in his second letter to the churches in Corinth using the analogy of sowing and reaping:

So I thought it necessary to urge the brothers to visit you in advance and finish the arrangements for the generous gift you had promised. Then it will be ready as a generous gift, not as one grudgingly given.

Remember this: whoever sows sparingly will also reap sparingly, and whoever sows generously will also reap generously.

(2 Corinthians 9:5-6)

As you read this, you may be feeling a bit uncomfortable. Uncomfortable because you don't tithe. It's not too late to start! Uncomfortable because you know God has prompted you to live a more generous life, and so far you have been disobedient… or maybe you're feeling uncomfortable because you've never really acknowledged that all you have, everything you own, is a gift from God, and you've never taken the time to say thank you.

Maybe you are at the other end of the scale and this is confirmation of a life lived with abundant generosity. If that is you, that's great!

Either way, my prayer for all of us is that we continue to grow in faith and generosity to such an extent that the world around us sits up and takes notice.

Questions

- Can you relate to the instructions Jesus gave to the twelve disciples, 'Freely you have received, freely give' (Matthew 10:8)?

- Was there anything in Malachi 3:6-10 that shocked or surprised you?

- In what ways is the freedom of New Covenant grace more challenging than the requirements of Old Testament laws?

- The financial plan of Sir John Laing was shared – have you ever applied something like this to aid your generosity?

- How do you feel about the amount of blessing we receive being in relation to the amount we give?

8
Miraculous Multiplication

There's a story reputed to be from a sermon delivered in December 1912 by Russell H Conwell, who was the pastor of Grace Baptist Church in Philadelphia. In his sermon he shares his encounter with a little girl named Hattie May Wiatt:

> Hattie May Wiatt, a six-year-old girl, lived near Grace Baptist Church in Philadelphia, USA. The Sunday school was very crowded. Russell H. Conwell, the minister, told her that one day they would have buildings big enough to allow everyone to attend. She said, 'I hope you will. It is so crowded I am afraid to go there alone.' He replied, 'When we get the money we will construct one large enough to get all the children in.'
>
> Two years later, in 1886, Hattie May died. After the funeral Hattie's mother gave the minister a little bag they had found under their daughter's pillow containing 57 cents in change that she had saved up. Alongside it was a note in her handwriting: 'To help build bigger so that more children can go to Sunday school.'

The minister changed all the money into pennies and offered each one for sale. He received $250 – and 54 of the cents were given back. The $250 was itself changed into pennies and sold by the newly formed 'Wiatt Mite Society'. In this way, her 57 cents kept on multiplying.

Twenty-six years later, in a talk entitled, 'The history of the 57 cents', the minister explained the results of her 57-cent donation: a church with a membership of over 5,600 people, a hospital where tens of thousands of people had been treated, 80,000 young people going through university, 2,000 people going out to preach the gospel – all this happened 'because Hattie May Wiatt invested her 57 cents'.[59]

What a story. With a little, a handful of coins saved by a young child, a property was purchased. It was a team effort and needed the whole body, but what an amazing achievement.

Only what is given away can God multiply

Within the questionnaire I circulated, one of the questions asked participants to share their favourite story about generosity. Here are two that relate directly to multiplication:

---

[59] www.accessinspiration.org/library/1863 (accessed 11th April 2024). 'Story related by Nicky Gumbel, Bible in One Year 2020, day 55 – Source: Hattie May Wiatt illustration from Sermon by Russell H Conwell 'The History of Fifty-Seven Cents', Sunday morning, December 1, 1912.

I chose to live by faith in my first ministry post. Prayed and sought God for provision and individuals started to bless us. I chose to tithe 10 per cent on everything – even a £10 gift. The generosity then came to me even more so. I was blessed with the rent on a flat, got given two cars and even had a gift of £1,000. We tithed on every monetary gift we received, which led us to believe God could provide anything. A few years later, we were blessed with the full deposit on a house (even after tithing on the gift), and were given a 300-seater chapel for our church (debt free and at no cost). Lots of little stories in one principle that we still live by today.

I preached about sowing 1 per cent of an idea that God gave you that you can't afford. A man in our church sowed his 1 per cent and had a 100 per cent plus harvest. His thank you to our church was to pay off our mortgage of $1.3 million.

I love stories from ordinary people, because if God is willing to use them, I feel encouraged that He'll use me.

For the same reason, I'm going to share a few biblical stories detailing God's abundant multiplication generosity. I hope this encourages you as our God is the same 'yesterday and today and for ever' (Hebrews 13:8). What He did then, He can do now.

What does Scripture tell us?

Most of us are familiar with the miracle of the feeding of the five thousand, or to be more accurate, when we include the women and children, the feeding of fifteen to twenty thousand:

Late in the afternoon the Twelve came to him and said, 'Send the crowd away so they can go to the surrounding villages and countryside and find food and lodging, because we are in a remote place here.'

He replied, 'You give them something to eat.'

They answered, 'We have only five loaves of bread and two fish – unless we go and buy food for all this crowd.' (About five thousand men were there.)

But he said to his disciples, 'Make them sit down in groups of about fifty each.' The disciples did so, and everyone sat down. Taking the five loaves and the two fish and looking up to heaven, he gave thanks and broke them. Then he gave them to the disciples to distribute to the people. They all ate and were satisfied, and the disciples picked up twelve basketfuls of broken pieces that were left over.
(Luke 9:12-17)

This is a miracle. God miraculously multiplied what was willingly given. There was no disputing, no rationalising what had happened; this was an unquestionable miracle.

In Matthew 15 we read that again Jesus miraculously multiplied the provisions, and fed four thousand, plus women and children, with only seven loaves and some fish. On the surface the similarities are astounding and a bit confusing. Why would the Gospel writers include such a similar miracle? Apart from numbers of people, loaves and fish, on the surface it appears like the same story. Wouldn't it have been better to use that precious ink and parchment to record a different miracle? We know there were lots of miracles to choose from, as John's Gospel tells us, 'Jesus did many other things as well. If every one of them were written down, I suppose that even the whole world would not have room for the books that would be written' (John 21:25).

With these two almost identical miracles, the importance comes when we look at the location. The feeding of the five thousand took place near Bethsaida, close to the Sea of Galilee. This was a Jewish area. Some commentators speculate that the five loaves, to feed five thousand, is reminiscent of the Pentateuch,[60] with the twelve baskets of leftovers alluding to the twelve tribes of Israel. In contrast, the feeding of the four thousand took place in the Decapolis, and was a predominantly Gentile area. In this miracle, seven loaves are used and seven baskets are collected. Some commentators believe this would have been important to the Gentiles, as the number seven was symbolic of completeness and evocative of the creation account.

This is interesting to us as yet again we have evidence that our amazing heavenly Father is always in the details. Here we have two almost identical miracles for two completely different groups of people that, when we look beyond the surface, have incredibly personal implications. This shouldn't surprise us; as we know, His every action and word testifies to the fact that His desire is that none shall perish.[61]

This is not a new strategy, as we see the miracle of multiplication recorded several times in the Old Testament:

---

[60] The foundational first five books of the Old Testament, said to be written by Moses.
[61] 2 Peter 3:9.

The wife of a man from the company of the prophets cried out to Elisha, 'Your servant my husband is dead, and you know that he revered the LORD. But now his creditor is coming to take my two boys as his slaves.'

Elisha replied to her, 'How can I help you? Tell me, what do you have in your house?'

'Your servant has nothing there at all,' she said, 'except a small jar of olive oil.'

Elisha said, 'Go round and ask all your neighbours for empty jars. Don't ask for just a few. Then go inside and shut the door behind you and your sons. Pour oil into all the jars, and as each is filled, put it to one side.'

She left him and shut the door behind her and her sons. They brought the jars to her and she kept pouring. When all the jars were full, she said to her son, 'Bring me another one.'

But he replied, 'There is not a jar left.' Then the oil stopped flowing.

She went and told the man of God, and he said, 'Go, sell the oil and pay your debts. You and your sons can live on what is left.'

(2 Kings 4:1-7)

As I read this, there are some immediate thoughts that spring to mind about how the woman might have felt and what we can learn.

To borrow vessels from her neighbours would have invited some awkward questions, but I wonder if it was important to God that she didn't just wish for help but was willing to step out in faith and receive it. Also, as the man of God, it would have been easy for Elisha to take over, but he made the woman pour out the oil as a sign of her trust and faithfulness in God, and so she understood this miracle was between her and God. What really amazes me, and is one of the thousands of questions I plan to ask when in heaven, is this: was the miracle given according to the measure of her previous faith in borrowing vessels? Had she borrowed more, would more would have been provided; had she gathered fewer jars, would less have been provided?

Later on in the same chapter we have another miracle of amazing, generous multiplication:

> A man came from Baal Shalishah, bringing the man of God twenty loaves of barley bread baked from the first ripe corn, along with some ears of new corn. 'Give it to the people to eat,' Elisha said.
>
> 'How can I set this before a hundred men?' his servant asked.
>
> But Elisha answered, 'Give it to the people to eat. For this is what the LORD says: "They will eat and have some left over."' Then he set it before them, and they ate and had some left over, according to the word of the LORD.
> (2 Kings 4:42-44)

Because the religion in the Northern Kingdom was apostate, the loaves, baked from the first fruits, had been brought by their owner to Elisha as the representative of God. Here God promises to not just provide, but to provide beyond the immediate need... miraculous multiplication.

And yet another:

Then the word of the LORD came to [Elijah]: 'Go at once to Zarephath in the region of Sidon and stay there. I have instructed a widow there to supply you with food.' So he went to Zarephath. When he came to the town gate, a widow was there gathering sticks. He called to her and asked, 'Would you bring me a little water in a jar so I may have a drink?' As she was going to get it, he called, 'And bring me, please, a piece of bread.'

'As surely as the LORD your God lives,' she replied, 'I don't have any bread – only a handful of flour in a jar and a little olive oil in a jug. I am gathering a few sticks to take home and make a meal for myself and my son, that we may eat it – and die.'

Elijah said to her, 'Don't be afraid. Go home and do as you have said. But first make a small loaf of bread for me from what you have and bring it to me, and then make something for yourself and your son. For this is what the LORD, the God of Israel, says: "The jar of flour will not be used up and the jug of oil will not run dry until the day the Lord sends rain on the land."'

She went away and did as Elijah had told her. So there was food every day for Elijah and for the woman and her family. For the jar of flour was not used up and the jug of oil did not run dry, in keeping with the word of the LORD spoken by Elijah.

(1 Kings 17:8-16)

In this piece of Scripture, Elijah is sent to the general region that Jezebel originated from, a place of potential danger, full of enemies, where loyalties to this evil queen may still be found, to be nourished by a widow – widowhood being a situation notorious for poverty in the ancient world.

In asking the widow to feed him first, Elijah is asking her to step out in faith. To risk starvation, to put her and her son's lives into God's hands and to trust that He would provide. Unsurprisingly, God doesn't let this widow down, and there is enough food for days.

What fantastic examples of miraculous multiplication!

Something out of nothing

If we truly believe that 'All Scripture is God-breathed and is useful for teaching, rebuking, correcting and training in righteousness' (2 Timothy 3:16), what can we learn from these miracles of multiplication?

For me it is clear that God is a master of multiplication, but He likes us to give Him something to work with. While we know God can make something out of nothing – He is, after all, God – in all the stories we have just looked at, He has asked for an offering. God is not restricted by numbers but is able to make our finances and resources stretch further than we could ever dream or imagine. In His hands what we have comes alive, it influences and becomes a messenger of the gospel. But in order for that to happen, we need to release it and give it to Him.

Also, in every story He asks those involved to step out in faith and partner with Him. Each time we step out in faith we take a risk. The disciples could have run out of food, the woman could have been left with lots of empty bottles, Elisha could have fed only a handful of men and the widow could have given her last meal to Elijah, sentencing herself and her son to an earlier death.

In all these accounts, God never lets His children down, but He does always require their participation. Don't you find this exciting? The creator of the universe wants to work with us. He wants to work with you and He wants to work with me. That's amazing.

I believe that God wants our finances to be multiplied. He will do this not only to encourage His children to be abundantly generous and to hold the things of this world lightly, but also as a way of witnessing to others and showing His power and majesty while signposting the way to His immense grace and mercy.

Questions

- What are your initial thoughts about God multiplying what we give? Has there been teaching in the past that has coloured your thoughts?

- Most of us are familiar with the two Gospel stories about feeding the four thousand and the five thousand. What does this tell us about God's intent?

- Can you remember a time when God has moved miraculously through your finances?

- Stories from the Old Testament about God's miraculous multiplication were shared within this chapter. Were there any elements that you feel aided or could have hindered the miraculous?

- How do you feel about the statement that 'in every story He asks those involved to step out in faith and partner with Him'. How willing are you to step out in faith in this area?

9

God, Is That You?

On a dark winter's night, a large American naval vessel encounters a bright light that appears to be on a collision course with the naval ship. Assuming this is an English vessel, the American captain establishes radio contact. The conversation goes like this:[62]

> Americans: 'Please divert your course 15 degrees to the north to avoid a collision.'
>
> English: 'Recommend you divert *your* course 15 degrees to the south to avoid a collision.'
>
> Americans: 'This is the captain of a US Navy ship. I say again, divert *your* course.'
>
> English: 'No, I say again, you divert *your* course.'
>
> Americans: 'This is the aircraft carrier USS *Abraham Lincoln*, the second largest ship in the United States' Atlantic fleet. We are accompanied by three destroyers, three cruisers and numerous support vessels. I demand that you change your course 15 degrees north. That's one-five degrees

---

[62] This a well-known story that can be found in different forms online. Original source unknown.

north, or counter measures will be undertaken to ensure the safety of this ship.'

English: 'This is a lighthouse. Your call.'

I have heard this story told twice, and both times it has made me laugh as I can identify with the American captain. In fact, there have been numerous times in my life where a conversation like this has occurred between me and God, with God ending the conversation by saying something along the lines of, 'I'm God, but it's your call.'

I'm guessing that I'm not the only one who's been there, who has felt prompted by the Holy Spirit to give a generous gift but has had an internal argument listing the reasons why the gift shouldn't be given. Maybe you've also heard God say, 'It's your call.'

How do we know that it is God prompting us to give generously?

When it comes to being a generous giver, there is a difference between knowledge and wisdom. Knowledge is all about the facts and can travel through borders, time, and even through generations via our DNA. The Knowledge Doubling Curve tells us, 'Until year 1900, human knowledge approximately doubled every century; by 1950, human knowledge doubled every 25 years; by 2000, human knowledge would double every year. Today, our knowledge is almost doubling every day!'[63]

---

[63] blogs.lse.ac.uk/usappblog/2017/09/23/thoughts-on-the-future-of-human-knowledge-and-machine-intelligence (accessed 15th September 2023).

We know more, but are we making better choices? Are we living more wisely? Are we being more obedient to God or hearing His voice more clearly?

This is where we need wisdom. Wisdom is all about what you do with the facts, how you live and the choices you make. Wisdom, and especially God's wisdom, empowers your knowledge, so you can be more effective in living a godly life.

We see this is in action in 1 Samuel 3:1-10:

> The boy Samuel ministered before the LORD under Eli. In those days the word of the LORD was rare; there were not many visions.
>
> One night Eli, whose eyes were becoming so weak that he could barely see, was lying down in his usual place. The lamp of God had not yet gone out, and Samuel was lying down in the house of the LORD, where the ark of God was. Then the LORD called Samuel.
>
> Samuel answered, 'Here I am.' And he ran to Eli and said, 'Here I am; you called me.'
>
> But Eli said, 'I did not call; go back and lie down.' So he went and lay down.
>
> Again, the LORD called, 'Samuel!' And Samuel got up and went to Eli and said, 'Here I am; you called me.'
>
> 'My son,' Eli said, 'I did not call; go back and lie down.'
>
> Now Samuel did not yet know the LORD: the word of the LORD had not yet been revealed to him.
>
> A third time the LORD called, 'Samuel!' And Samuel got up and went to Eli and said, 'Here I am; you called me.'

Then Eli realised that the LORD was calling the boy. So Eli told Samuel, 'Go and lie down, and if he calls you, say, "Speak, LORD, for your servant is listening."' So, Samuel went and lay down in his place.

The LORD came and stood there, calling as at the other times, 'Samuel! Samuel!'

Then Samuel said, 'Speak, for your servant is listening.'

Samuel knew that someone was speaking to him but, even though he 'ministered before the LORD', he didn't have the wisdom to know who the voice belonged to. What we do know from Scripture is that the voice was so real that Samuel believed it was Eli speaking. Whether Samuel heard the audible voice of God or if it was an 'inner' voice, Scripture doesn't elaborate.

Just like most parents can hear their own child's voice above a cacophony of chaos, with experience and guidance from the Holy Spirit, we learn to recognise the voice of God. Sometimes, though, we may need the input of another to help bring clarification and much-needed wisdom.

The help of another

Many years ago, we were blessed to holiday on a Caribbean island. At the time our daughter hadn't been born and our boys were ten and thirteen years old. Towards the end of our holiday, we attended an organised excursion. For lunch we were taken to a picture-perfect cove where the sand was golden and the sea was as clear as glass. On the beach there were a few women selling homemade jewellery. I had browsed the stall, listened to people bartering and, against my better judgement and desire to help, decided that I didn't want or, more specifically, need anything. Partly this was because a few hours earlier we had given a large sum of money to a local family, and I felt that was probably good enough. Our abundantly generous God had other ideas.

Reece, our persuasive eldest son, begged me to buy something from these ladies, as we had seen some of the humbler living conditions on the island, and his heart had been touched. Together we approached the stall and I asked for his help in choosing something. When I asked for his help, I hadn't realised the extent to which his heart had been impacted as he didn't choose one piece of jewellery, but an earrings, necklace and bracelet set! While it was possibly the most expensive thing on the table, it was still easily affordable. To encourage his sense of justice, which is still strong, I agreed that I'd get the whole set and asked him what price I should try to buy it for. Everyone who had bought something had bartered and bought at a much lower price. To my surprise, he requested that I pay the full price as we had the means to do so. I agreed, purchased the jewellery set (which I still own) and before we had even made it back to our place on the beach, the ladies who managed the stall had packed up and were on their way home. The purchase, which had little financial impact on me, had made a huge difference to them.

Matthew 13:12 (NLT) tells us:

> To those who listen to my teaching, more understanding will be given, and they will have an

abundance of knowledge. But for those who are not listening, even what little understanding they have will be taken away from them.

In this instance I needed someone else, my son, to confirm God's voice that was encouraging me to buy and be generous with my purchase. This was a pivotal moment in my faith journey and helped hone my ears to recognise God's voice.

At other times we need to simply say, 'Speak, Lord, for your servant is listening,' and take ourselves away to a quiet place where His voice can be clearly heard without the noisy and disruptive interruptions that come from the busyness of life. When we look through Scripture, we can see God has a history of meeting His people in silent moments, encourages the practice of silence, and even retreated to find silence Himself.

Jesus promised that 'My sheep hear My voice' (John 10:27, NKJV). If we are to hear His voice, it stands to reason He is speaking to us – the real question is, are we listening? I'm guessing it will be different for everyone, but for me the inner voice of God isn't pushy or cajoling but is clear and confident.

The book of James describes it this way: 'But the wisdom that comes from heaven is first of all pure; then peace-loving, considerate, submissive, full of mercy and good fruit, impartial and sincere' (James 3:17).

If you are one of His sheep, then He is speaking to you. However, the fact that God speaks does not ensure that we will hear correctly. There have been times I have got it wrong, when I have moved generously and have been taken advantage of. I have accepted this, forgiven myself and anyone else involved and viewed this as an essential part of my discipleship training. The times I get it wrong are becoming fewer, and I am getting better at being able to distinguish the voice of the true Shepherd. Without time and experience, this wouldn't happen. As a friend has often said, 'I would rather be told off by Jesus for being too generous than admonished for being stingy.' A sentiment I wholeheartedly agree with!

How else can we hear the voice of God?

From my own experience, when God speaks it will be in a way that is unique to the person and the situation. I shared how God used Reece to prompt me to buy the jewellery. In the same way God has used others to bring about this book.

Initially God spoke to me at a conference through the key speaker, who shared that he felt God was telling him there was someone listening who was being nudged by God to write a book. To be honest, I wasn't even in the conference tent but a few hundred feet away, snug in a caravan with our daughter. But through the immense power and sheer volume of the speakers, I could hear every word. When my husband returned to our caravan, the first thing he said was, 'There's been a word for you.' This was confirmation of what I already knew.

For years I didn't do anything with this word as nothing felt right. I wasn't sure what type of book God wanted me to write or what type of book I was capable of writing. So I waited and prayed, constantly questioning if I'd heard wrongly.

Several years later, I awoke one morning with the strangest word on my lips: 'unifundshe'. As I'm a professional fundraiser, I broke the word down and reasoned this must be a fund for girls who were at university, and for some bizarre reason I had been dreaming about it. However, the word stayed with me, hovering on the outskirts of my brain.

Two weeks later I flew to Kenya with a group from Compassion UK.[64] Towards the end of the week, we attended a lovely, Holy Spirit-filled church in a slum area. The pastor explained that the worship would all be in Swahili, with the words on the screen, and to pronounce it 'as we see it'. To my immense surprise, a few songs in, the word 'unifundshe' appeared, which I later discovered means 'teach me'. After praying this through, I took this as confirmation that God wanted me to write a book that would build and teach His people.

You'd think that after a word from a guest speaker, confirmation from my husband and a dream that linked to worship in a different country, I'd be desperate to write the book that God had commissioned me to write. The problem was I lacked direction, and despite the number of times God had spoken to me, I began to have doubts.

Then one day we were with friends at a farm. Even though this was a couple we have known and loved for a long time, I hadn't shared any of my book journey with them. From nowhere, while admiring the piglets, the husband asked me, 'When are you going to write a book?' Even while I was telling him that not everyone has a book

---

[64] Compassion is a Christian child-sponsorship organisation: www.compassionuk.org (accessed 3rd April 2024).

in them, I knew this was another God prompt. I'm aware this story doesn't show me in a good light (thankfully I've never pretended to be perfect), but it does show the many ways God will speak to us.

When we look at Scripture, God has spoken through a donkey, through angels, visions, dreams, symbolic actions and miraculous signs revealing His purposes so we know how He wants us to partner with Him. For many of us, He may have spoken through a friend, prayer, circumstances or the church.

What can we learn from others?

Over the years, I have helped raise millions of pounds by asking thousands of people to support many good causes. Some have responded immediately; others have needed time to come to a decision. Both avenues, in seeking to hear from God and be obedient to Him, are valid and good.

Part of the reason I circulated the questionnaire is that there is deep wisdom in the body of Christ. It is often the unsung heroes we can learn great lessons from. Here is how some of those heroes responded to the question, 'Based on your experience, how would you suggest godly wisdom should be applied when practising financial generosity?'

It is the attitude of our hearts that is most important. Obedience gets us into the zone, but it is our heart motivation that should determine how much we give.

We do need to be wise – God is not asking everyone to give everything away (only one man in the Bible); however, faith should be applied to giving as well so that we don't just stay within a limit.

Considering whether giving simply 'maintains' the problem or will bring transformation.

Godly wisdom is necessary when giving money away, as it is not right to waste God's provision in the wrong way. We should first pray into our motive for giving and if it is God's will, we will know a peace about it.

Godly wisdom is being able to look past our situations and remain in peace, knowing we are taken care of. But it starts with obedience to His Word.

Listening to what God tells you and obeying is true wisdom. Stewardship is important but can often be a term used to justify stinginess and a poverty spirit. Likewise, 'logic' can be used to mask fear. Godly wisdom recognises that God has provided all and that if He asks us to give, He will continue to provide for us. He tells us to trust Him with our money, and He will prove His generosity to us.

Godly wisdom is about responding to the prompting of the Holy Spirit; when He prompts, we respond… it may rarely seem like human wisdom, yet the outcome demonstrates far beyond the seen. (Kingdom outcomes.)

Prayer, prayer and prayer! What does God's Word say? When you feel God's prompting, do it even if it makes no sense to you. Remember it all comes from Him anyway. Don't look for man's praise; just be obedient to Him.

Giving out of the abundance of your heart. Give as you feel led by the Holy Spirit and not because you feel pressured to do so against your will.

Giving that grows from a healthy relationship makes a lot of sense in most instances. Know who we are supporting by our giving or having taken time to research why our giving to a particular cause is important. Also, what we are giving to is important – especially as we are stewards of what we have and what we give!

Through prayer and good knowledge of what you are giving to.

However God speaks to you, whenever He prompts you to give generously, this is a moment for you to step out in faith, to be bold, to be brave, to nail your colours to the mast and decide what you really believe about God, and act on it.

Questions

- Are you able to identify with Samuel in the story regarding his difficulty in recognising God's voice?

- Can you describe a time when you have known God is prompting you to do or give? How did He do this and how did you feel?

- What were the results of this prompting?

- Just like with the jewellery purchase, can you recall a time when you have needed the input of another to help bring about clarification and much-needed wisdom regarding a financial decision?

- Do you resonate or disagree with the responses given to the questionnaire? Why/Why not?

10
Is Generosity the New Evangelism?

I want to begin by sharing a unique gift I have. This gift has evolved over time; maybe some of you also have this gift, or a similar one. My gift is the ability to recognise certain things about the sectors or accents I'm submerged in.

I know that doesn't sound particularly impressive; it's not like I'm telling you I can travel through time or read minds. But before you discount my gift entirely, let me elaborate a bit. I spent the first sixteen years of my life living in an inner-city council estate called Custom House, situated in the East End of London. This wasn't a huge estate and it was nestled between two others, Beckton and Canning Town. To the front of the estate was the A13 motorway and to the back were the Victoria and Albert Docks.

My gift was that I could spot the Custom House accent, not the East End cockney accent, but the Custom House accent, for years. I could tell the difference between that and any other London accent; for me the Custom House accent stood alone and was instantly recognisable.

I haven't lived in Custom House for a few decades, and as I mentioned, my gift has evolved. I'm now immersed in the charity and Christian world and can normally spot a charity worker or Christian immediately, based on their choice of clothes, stance and language. What a gift! Not sure where or when I'll ever use this gift, but a gift is a gift, thanks be to God. And the reason I share that is, just as I could distinguish a Custom House accent from any other, or pick out a Christian or charity worker, people should be able to tell that we are followers of Jesus by how we live. As it is explained so eloquently in the book *Being Human*:

> We are made in the image of God, we are His image bearers, a representation of God on earth. Our very words, actions and behaviours should be a signpost to the One who made us as He has crowned us with glory and honour.[65]

Because of this, at the very least others should question what is different about us. And part of that difference should be generous, loving evangelism.

Selfless concern

The mark of generous, loving evangelism is true, selfless concern for others' physical, material, psychological and spiritual needs. We are blessed in having many amazing Christian organisations that do that. Organisations such as Christians Against Poverty that have seen more than eight

---

[65] Jo Frost and Peter Lynas, *Being Human* (London: Hodder & Stoughton, 2023), p 16.

thousand people make a response to Jesus since 2010.[66] Or the team at Prison Fellowship who, in 2023 alone, shared the love of Jesus with 29,159 prisoners.[67] Transforming Lives for Good is another great charity that in one year connected, supported and shared the gospel with 5,454 children.[68] These organisations, through social initiatives and outstanding generosity, are seeing people turn to Christ.

This is wonderful, but it's just the tip of the iceberg. There are thousands of churches, individuals and organisations that generously reach out in love to those in their community. They are generously serving and giving in ways that make others question their motives and open the doors for them to explain about the love of Jesus. Often this avenue to serve is only possible through the gift of giving generously.

As someone who is part of a church that wholeheartedly serves their local community and walks with others who are doing the same, I know it isn't always easy. Sometimes the immediate result doesn't seem to justify the financial cost or volunteer hours. You can be left questioning if you've wasted resources and time. It's in moments like these that we need to have faith and trust in God.

I know a lovely gentleman who even in his eighties has a deep gratitude, loyalty and affection for The Salvation Army because of a Christmas food hamper his family received when he was a child. Although he didn't start

[66] www.capuk.org/about-us/our-impact (accessed 19th January 2024).
[67] www.prisonfellowship.org.uk (accessed 19th January 2024).
[68] www.tlg.org.uk/about-us/tlg-impact (accessed 22nd January 2024).

attending church until he was an adult, he cites this occasion as his introduction to Jesus. Those in The Salvation Army who bought, packed and delivered the hamper that served as the starting point for his journey may never have been aware of the seeds they sowed or the impact they had.

I want to suggest that when we look at Scripture, generous, loving evangelism wasn't restricted to a sweet, sentimental feeling or an annual event. It meant action, feeling the cost, stepping out in faith, getting your hands dirty and inserting love into real-world activities.

We see this in Acts 2:42-47:

> They devoted themselves to the apostles' teaching and to fellowship, to the breaking of bread and to prayer. Everyone was filled with awe at the many wonders and signs performed by the apostles. All the believers were together and had everything in common. They sold property and possessions to give to anyone who had need. Every day they continued to meet together in the temple courts. They broke bread in their homes and ate together with glad and sincere hearts, praising God and enjoying the favour of all the people. And the Lord added to their number daily those who were being saved.

For the first church, generous, loving evangelism came at a great financial cost as they 'sold property and possessions to give to anyone who had need'. We know that sharing was a cultural normality within Middle Eastern culture. However, in the Greco-Roman culture, sharing possessions was limited to those of equal social status. In this piece of Scripture, we find followers of Jesus being called to a higher standard, a new level of generosity, as 'anyone' included Diaspora Jews,[69] Galilean disciples and apostles and urban Jerusalemites, both wealthy and poor. This different behaviour was attractional to others and we read that 'the Lord added to their number daily those who were being saved'.

This is reinforced through the writings of one of the early Church Fathers, Tertullian,[70] where he describes how those in the local community were influenced by the generosity they saw on a daily basis. This was during a time in history when opposition to Christianity and the Church was intensifying, and becoming a follower of Christ was a potentially dangerous decision. Although an apologist, Tertuillan was quick to point out that it wasn't any particular theological or philosophical argument that would ultimately persuade people of the truth about Jesus. Rather it was the unusual behaviour that captivated non-Christians. In one memorable statement, Tertullian said this: 'It is mainly the deeds of a love so noble that lead many to put a brand upon us. *See*, they say, *how they love one another* ... how they are ready even to die for one another'![71]

Hands-on love in action inserted into real-life activities.

In the Talking Jesus research, which explores the faith landscape within the UK, when non-Christians were asked to describe the Christians they knew, the three

---

[69] Those who had remained in Jerusalem after Pentecost (Acts 2:9-11).

[70] He was born in Carthage, and lived approximately AD 155-160.

[71] www.logoslibrary.org/tertullian/apology/39.html (accessed 24th January 2024).

most popular responses were caring, friendly and good-humoured.[72] That's so uplifting! As most of the Christians I know have these three characteristics, I am in strong agreement with this summary.

However, in the same survey, the two top descriptions to describe the UK Church were hypocritical and narrow minded.[73] With more food banks in the UK than a certain well-known fast-food chain,[74] and with most of them operating from churches, and considering that church buildings create £55.7 billion in value per year (which is twice as much as the total spend on adult social care by local authorities),[75] maybe some of our churches need a public relations makeover?

These findings do make me question whether we need to investigate how we personalise and humanise the generosity of the Church. We know the Church does amazing work, and while this isn't done in the pursuit of reward, we want to ensure there are no barriers, real or perceived, to sharing the gospel. Ideally, we want the generosity we extend to have the same or greater impact it did during Tertullian's time. We want people to know the hope, grace and love there is in being a child of God. For many of us, our desire is for others to know the

---

[72] www.eauk.org/assets/files/downloads/Talking-Jesus-Report.pdf (accessed 15th October 2023), p 17.

[73] www.eauk.org/assets/files/downloads/Talking-Jesus-Report.pdf (accessed 15th October 2023), p 18.

[74] www.fullfact.org/electionlive/2019/dec/9/food-banks-more-mcdonalds (accessed 25th September 2023).

[75] www.nationalchurchestrust.org/sites/default/files/GADS1597%20%E2%80%93%20NCT%20House%20of%20Good%202021%20V7%20SINGLE-PAGES.pdf (accessed 16th July 2024), p 5.

empowering of the Holy Spirit and, upon leaving earth, to spend eternity in heaven.

This is controversial, but at times I wonder if we need to question: if our activities are not making Jesus known, overtly or subtly, are they a good use of time and resources? To begin answering that question, let's dive into the scripture where we read Jesus says, 'A new command I give you: love one another' (John 13:34). Our responsibility to love one another is a commandment, not a suggestion, good advice or one among many options from which we can choose. Jesus is commanding us to do something. We are subject to the authority of Jesus Christ. We are not the masters of our own lives. We are not free to live however we please. Jesus tells us, 'If you love me, keep my commands' (John 14:15), and, 'You are my friends if you do what I command' (John 15:14).

So if we struggle with the idea that we've been saved by grace but must obey the commandments, the passage in John 13 will really annoy us. What may annoy us even more is that this isn't strictly a new command. In Leviticus 19:17-18 God spoke to the children of Israel and said:

> Do not hate a fellow Israelite in your heart. Rebuke your neighbour frankly so that you will not share in their guilt.
> Do not seek revenge or bear a grudge against anyone among your people, but love your neighbour as yourself. I am the LORD.

Clearly the newness of the command to love isn't in the command itself, but in the depth that we are called to love. As children of God sitting under New Covenant grace, there is a greater expectation. Never in the history of humankind had God appeared in human flesh and demonstrated His love for humanity by sacrificing Himself on a cross so that they might live for ever. If that fact doesn't blow your mind, nothing will. Quite simply, this monumental moment in history has forever changed how we love each other. It has also changed how we measure success and determine what activities are worthy of our time and resources.

The 2021 Census tells us that for the first time the number of Christians in the UK has dropped below 50 per cent.[76] And of this 50 per cent, only 6 per cent attend church, read their Bibles and pray regularly.[77] In seemingly stark contrast, by 2050 Pew Research predicts Christianity will remain the largest belief system on earth. That's exciting! It's more exciting for the East and Global South as the predictions are based on 40 per cent of global Christians being African and half the country of China bowing the knee to Jesus.[78]

The predictions for the UK are not quite as positive, and that's where we need people to see something different about the followers of Jesus. That's where we need to be people who move in abundant generosity; individuals who don't hoard but hold what they own with open arms, willing to release it for the good of His kingdom.

---

[76] www.ons.gov.uk/peoplepopulationandcommunity/culturalidentity/religion/bulletins/religionenglandandwales/census2021 (accessed 11th April 2024).

[77] www.eauk.org/assets/files/downloads/Talking-Jesus-Report.pdf (accessed 15th October 2023), p 6.

[78] www.pewresearch.org/religion/2015/04/02/religious-projections-2010-2050 (accessed 18th October 2023).

Because we serve the living God, the above figures do not concern me, as the kingdom of Christ is unique and God will continue to build His Church. However, the above figures do remind me this is not a time for Christians to blend in; rather, it is a time for them to stand out.

It is a time for our difference to be noticed.

Salt and light

Matthew 5:13-16 tells us:

> You are the salt of the earth. But if the salt loses its saltiness, how can it be made salty again? It is no longer good for anything, except to be thrown out and trampled underfoot.
>
> You are the light of the world. A town built on a hill cannot be hidden. Neither do people light a lamp and put it under a bowl. Instead they put it on its stand, and it gives light to everyone in the house. In the same way, let your light shine before others, that they may see your good deeds and glorify your Father in heaven.

Salt and light may seem everyday and a bit insignificant, but by their nature they spread their influence far and wide. The greatest need, the biggest call on Christians going forward, is to be distinctively ourselves; to be a group of people who unashamedly follow Jesus' commands and love like He loved us; that, by the very nature of being countercultural but also appealing, we become people of influence.

In 2 Corinthians 9:13-14 Paul tells us:

Because of the service by which you have proved yourselves, others will praise God for the obedience that accompanies your confession of the gospel of Christ, and for your generosity in sharing with them and with everyone else. And in their prayers for you their hearts will go out to you, because of the surpassing grace God has given you.

Here, generosity is not just sharing possessions, but has opened the door to sharing the gospel. Generosity should never be used to manipulate, although it does offer one of the most powerful ways to leverage the blessings of God for the advancement of the kingdom.

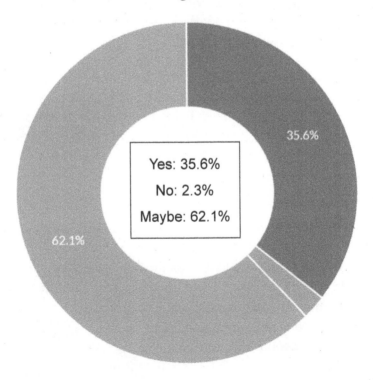

Yes: 35.6%
No: 2.3%
Maybe: 62.1%

In the survey that was circulated, 62 per cent answered 'maybe' to the question, 'In your experience is generosity an effective evangelism method?' and 35 per cent voted 'yes'.

This is a hard question to answer. There have been more times than I want to recall when I have been financially generous and several years down the line that individual is seemingly no nearer to Jesus. Recently I asked a homeless man to accompany me to a famous coffee shop so I could buy him a hot drink and something to eat. He walked with me to the coffee shop then excused himself and speed-walked away! We can't control others' responses to our generosity, but we can be people who respond generously to others.

Some of the reasons for the above response to the questionnaire are listed below:

Generosity is countercultural so when we express God's nature by being generous, we present a different approach to life and thus an opportunity to share the gospel in words as well as works.

I feel it's a lifestyle attraction thing. People are attracted by generosity (don't mean financial necessarily) and so [it] gives the opportunity for deeper conversations.

Our local church meets a lot of practical needs in our community via the generosity of our attendees. So many times members of our local community have been bowled over when we have been able to help out and often ask, 'Why?' or, 'What's the catch?' This is often a huge open door to the gospel (we give because we have been given to).

We are called to share the gospel and talk about Jesus as the Bread of life. But people need bread as well.

The money you give is like planting a seed.

The world notices when generosity is shown. Financial or time. Helping people when they have a need is priceless.

It can help create a connection but needs to be done sensitively and without any risk of being patronising. Otherwise it can actually be counterproductive as pride and shame can pull the recipient away from you.

One or two times I've been generous with people who do not know Jesus and it has caused curiosity or exploration. Most of the time, though, people just think I'm being nice.

People can be moved when they are blessed by others with no agenda.

When you give expecting nothing in return, you are displaying love to the recipient. This can lead to trust and the opportunity to speak God's truth into their life. 'People don't care what you know until they know that you care.'

I think the way we treat money is a powerful apologetic to a watching world.

Irrespective of whether we believe generosity is the new evangelism or the same behaviours under a different name, when we act with generosity for the benefit of others, it offers the recipient and those watching a clear picture of Christ, who at the cross gave His life and all He had so that we might find life for ever. This is the ultimate act of generosity from which everything else must flow.

144

Questions

- Are there any accents or people groups that you can immediately distinguish? Why is this?

- Do you agree with the statement, 'The mark of generous, loving evangelism is true, selfless concern for others' physical, material, psychological and spiritual needs'? How do you live this out?

- What jumps out to you from Acts 2:42-47? What are the parallels to the behaviour we read about in this portion of Scripture and the chapter title 'Is Generosity the New Evangelism?'?

- How do you feel about the Talking Jesus research, 2021 Census and predictions from Pew Research?

- If asked, 'In your experience is generosity an effective evangelism method?', what would be your response and why?

Conclusion

Let me congratulate you on finishing this book! Especially as this isn't just any book; it's one that has encouraged you on every page to give your money away and to let go of that which you have earned, for the benefit of His kingdom, therefore putting your trust in Him above yourself. This is tough, countercultural, radical thinking. This is the type of behaviour that indicates a deeper level of discipleship and could start a much-needed revival. Let me hear you say, 'Yes and amen!'

Throughout the whole process of writing the manuscript on my computer to holding a tangible item, my dream has been that this book will be guided by the Holy Spirit into the right hands; right now, those hands are yours. My hope is that Christians will embrace a financially generous outlook, increase their level of generosity to a lavish level or encourage others on their giving journey, the outcome being that the escalation in loving and giving generously will become impossible to ignore as organisations, churches and individuals are able to impact immeasurably more with the grace and hope of knowing Jesus.

If you find this a bit heavy and overwhelming, take comfort in this Russian folk tale:

Once upon a time two mice were sitting watching the snow fall and settle on the branch of a tree. The first mouse asked, 'How much does a snowflake weigh?' The second mouse replied, 'A little less than nothing.'

The mice continued to watch the snow falling. Eventually, the snowflakes lessened and then they stopped. A final snowflake fell onto the branch of the tree. The branch creaked, snapped and fell to the ground. The first mouse exclaimed, 'So, a little less than nothing can make a big difference!'

'So as we can see,' said the second mouse, 'the lessons are clear. Always do what you can to help as little things can make a big difference.'[79]

As I have noted, 'God loves a cheerful giver' (2 Corinthians 9:7), and my prayer is any changes you make to your giving will be done wholeheartedly and joyfully. Together we can achieve so much and make a humongous difference. If each person does what they are able, not only will they feel better about themselves and move closer to God, but they'll also impact the world they inhabit. To reference Scripture, a few loaves and fishes went a long way after they were blessed by Jesus.

To kickstart this new phase of your giving adventure, you could start by reviewing your budget and increasing your tithe, or embarking on 'The Thirty-day Generosity Challenge' (see Appendix 3). Only you know what deeper level God is calling you into.

---

[79] Source unknown.

However you decide to give, I want to assure you of my encouragement.

Enjoy the journey!

Appendix 1
Results of the Questionnaire

The questionnaire was sent in November 2022 to approximately seventy people, stating, 'While I am aware there are numerous ways to be generous, this survey focuses solely on financial generosity.' Of those seventy, fifty kind souls responded – thank you!

As not every comment could make it in to the main body of the book, but every comment was valid, I thought you may want to read through the results and soak in the collective wisdom.

Enjoy!

Q1 On a scale of 1-10 (1 being low, 10 being high) how generous would you rate yourself?

Average answer:
7.32

Q2 How would you describe generosity?

Answers:

Giving of time, talent and finances.

Giving of time, money, acts of service – but primarily money.

Giving in a way that falls outside what the person expects or asks for, or which results in you making a sacrifice when giving the gift rather than you benefiting from it (ie tax avoidance, gaining a positive reputation).

Sacrificial and including time as well as financial.

Big heart, share resources, create shortcuts for others, generous with time. Give to local church and to a number of mission opportunities and spontaneously when I see a need.

A recognition of all that God has given me and a desire to be part of His provision to others.

Giving away freely from the good that God has given to me for the sake of others, and for His glory.

Going above and beyond to help those who need you. Being generous with words, time, skills, abilities and finance.

Generosity is about giving to God and giving to others out of the blessing we have been given. It's about sharing our resources with open hands.

Giving financially but also in time and acts of service.

Giving to others/meeting the needs of others/putting others' needs first.

Give to Christian charities and missionaries plus non-Christian organisations. Give as led.

Giving away when you don't necessarily have the means to do so.

A natural part of the Christian life.

Giving of time, resources and money to others in need, or just to show love, joyfully, modestly without expecting anything in return.

Giving without counting the cost.

Being ready and willing to share your financial resources with those around you.

Recognising everything we have is God-given and using the money you have to bless others.

Giving without any thought for yourself or for the thought that the recipients owe you or are in your debt. When we give we should be seeking the smile of God.

Giving when you can least afford it.

Generosity comes in many forms. Giving something freely that you have to someone else.

Selflessly giving to benefit the lives of others.

Regular tithing. Giving to charities – secular and Christian. Giving to individuals if a need is noted.

Giving my time or money to others who are in need, or not. Giving selflessly and giving everything you have.

Giving to bless others, whether they need it or not, from what I have, whether I can afford it or not. This being as a result of God's incredible generosity to us.

It's an attitude first, and an action second. It starts in the heart and travels to the head and gut!

Giving what you have or don't have a lot of. You can at times go without to make sure someone has. Generosity comes in various ways, time, finance, emotional support.

Giving beyond what can be seen. Generosity = Cost.

Choosing to give (anything) to someone else without much in it for self.

A practical demonstration of love.

Generosity is unexpectedly giving to others to meet a need or bring a blessing. Expecting nothing in return.

Sharing of what we have, hold and are given with the world around us.

Generosity is freely giving to others through time, touch, talent and treasure.

Giving what God has given you to bless or help someone else.

Being ready to give to every good cause on every occasion.

Meeting the needs of others and not just self.

Sacrificial giving.

I would say it's an attitude of heart. Generosity is about being obedient with what God has given you in its fullest sense.

A giving of yourself, time and resources to another.

Giving sacrificially when you see a need or are inspired by God to give.

Being guided to give through an open heart with an informed and humble attitude to meet the needs of others. Generosity starts with gratitude and overflows as compassion, whether it is giving time, love or money.

By meeting a need of a person in need. Also giving more than they were expecting.

I give when I feel called to give.

The act of giving your time, resources, money, etc to someone who needs it.

Commitment to 10 per cent of net income plus ad hoc gifts to emergencies. Offering accommodation to people in need (currently a Ukrainian family). Working for a lower income in the charitable sector rather than seeking income as a priority.

Going over and above what is expected, especially if done anonymously.

My wife and I have loved giving. We have always tithed to local church and given to individuals and ministries as led.

Giving beyond obligation.

Giving of oneself.

Generosity is open-handed and selfless willingness to ensure that others are completely swamped by abundance.

Q3 Do you think practising generosity is an important part of the Christian discipleship journey?

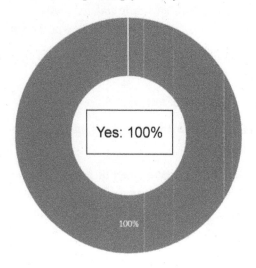

Q4 In your experience is generosity an effective evangelism method?

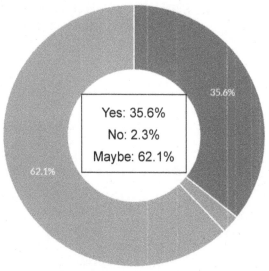

Q5 Can you elaborate on your answer for the previous question (please feel free to share an example)?

Answers:

What we call the social gospel, of feeding and visiting the poor, are all footsteps to the gospel message.

Any disciple of Jesus Christ should be generous and, in some instances, this will trigger people to ask, 'Why?' and therefore an opportunity to explain. Also the church supporting the community as a collective hardship fund not just for the congregation. 'The church helped me when...'

It can be if other people see you practise it, but partly generosity should be hidden in order to avoid being generous for the benefits that it gives you. Being both gracious and generous I think is noticeable.

I don't see giving as a tool of evangelism. It is part of our worship and service to the Lord. I suppose I also see it as a responsibility. A responsibility to give from our plenty to those who are serving us (eg church leadership) and those that are struggling.

A gift opens the way for the giver! People want to be around people with a generous heart.

Generosity is countercultural so when we express God's nature by being generous, we present a different approach to life and thus an opportunity to share the gospel in words as well as works.

In times of adversity or need, generous Christians represent the heart of a generous God.

I feel it's a lifestyle attraction thing. People are attracted by generosity (don't mean financial necessarily) and so it gives the opportunity for deeper conversations.

Our local church meets a lot of practical needs in our community via the generosity of our attendees. So many times members of our local community have been bowled over when we have been able to help out and often ask, 'Why?' or, 'What's the catch?' This is often a huge open door to the gospel (we give because we have been given to).

If you can be generous towards a non-Christian you witness Christ to them.

People are amazed that strangers would give them something free.

Help support ... organisations that are involved with promoting training for evangelism.

We are called to share the gospel and talk about Jesus as the Bread of life. But people need bread as well.

Can't think of any specific examples, hence the maybe, but I act that way.

People these days need to feel loved before we get the right to talk about who God is and what He means to us.

I feel cautious about the definition of the phrase 'effective evangelism method'. I'd agree that living generously, being a quick and regular giver to others, is a way of sharing God's love, and it's the sort of thing that gets noticed and appreciated. More radical acts of generosity can prompt discussions about the motivations for them.

Yes, a lady I used to work with was having major financial problems and I collected £250 from my Christian friends to help her out. She couldn't believe the kindness and was very tearful. She could not understand how we would give without hesitation and she could not understand why we didn't require the money back. I was able to witness to her over a period of time and felt I had opened a door to the gospel through giving.

We can't 'buy' anyone into believing in God but we can provide the finances to support those who are witnessing and working in the mission field, home or away.

The money you give is like planting a seed.

Our actions will reach people more deeply than our words. Even though we mean well, we can easily offend and make the situation worse. If we are genuine with our actions and generosity flows from the heart, the world would receive it better.

The world notices when generosity is shown. Financial or time. Helping people when they have a need: priceless.

Food banks, the heart system in the café, giving baby clothes to those who need them, giving away things you simply don't need to bless others. The way you give something and how it opens a conversation is how it begins good evangelism to others. Why have you given this to me? It is so generous, because I believe that Jesus would do the same.

It can help create a connection but needs to be done sensitively and without any risk of being patronising. Otherwise it can actually be counterproductive as pride and shame can pull the recipient away from you.

Generosity needs to be unconditional – making it a part of evangelism has a touch of coercion about it! The best evangelism is people who model their faith through their lives.

Christianity is all about generosity. For God so loved the world He gave His only Son. Our way to people is by giving.

God gave us Jesus, there can be no greater model of generosity. Generosity is at the heart of the gospel.

One or two times I've been generous with people who do not know Jesus and it has caused curiosity or exploration. Most of the time, though, people just think I'm being nice.

People can be moved when they are blessed by others with no agenda.

When you give expecting nothing in return you are displaying love to the recipient. This can lead to trust and the opportunity to speak God's truth into their life. 'People don't care what you know until they know that you care.'

It depends on the context I think, a lot of the gold of generosity is in its secrecy/discreetness, such as financial giving to causes we're passionate about. However, being generous in all sorts of ways to those around us in need can be a powerful example of love.

I believe followers of Jesus should be the most generous people on the face of the earth. The Bible talks about giving more than 2,000 times and not always in the context of money. As we live a generous life looking to bless others with no expectation to receive back, it speaks of God's heart. Generosity is in His DNA and it should be in ours. Also, the book of Proverbs says the generous will be happy and blessed [for example, Proverbs 11:25]. As we're generous, others will take note and ask why.

The world of the righteous grows larger and larger, right? I believe that where our treasure is there our heart is also; if we 'invest' in people financially it reaps reward.

When you show generosity to others, they are much more open to listen to you, and as the saying goes, actions speak louder than words.

People don't care how much you know till they know how much you care.

I guess it can be in the right setting; context and delivery are key. The motivation – the why, who and how it is done in a sensitive way.

I think the way we treat money is a powerful apologetic to a watching world.

Giving opens doors to answer the question, 'Why did you give to me?'

Generosity is never a transaction; it is an indication of our heart of compassion. Emotional generosity is limited to feelings, hence it is seldom true that generosity is always the most effective tool to advance or aid our evangelism. It may be a contributing factor, but is not enough in itself. Compassion is greater than simple passion to fuel our generosity. Compassion is passion with a willingness to become a 'companion' in solving a need or giving support in any way required.

I have had work done before and paid above what I was charged. This led to them asking why I was being so generous and I could share that God blesses me so why shouldn't I bless others. Being generous can open so many doors to sharing the gospel.

I have given food, money, car lifts to friends and it helps them to see a difference in me and therefore the generosity of God through me.

Words and deeds together, not one without the other!

Well, it certainly enables things to happen that would otherwise be impossible. There is a dimension to it when people ask questions about why we are generous, eg, it is noticeable in the town where I live that a significant number of those offering accommodation to Ukrainian families are church folk. Having said that, the confidentiality we seek in relation to giving does mitigate against this on a personal basis.

Providing a good example to others is a valuable form of witness.

I think giving time, talents or money can be a practical demonstration of God's love to another. This action can open a person's heart to knowing God.

Sometimes giving generously results in being taken advantage of without the recipient having any intention of seeking Christ.

I think giving can make people open.

Our church has been able to donate more than £250,000 over the last nine years, making a big and direct difference to the effectiveness of a large number of Christian ministries large and small; and across the whole range of local, national and international contexts. Generosity has been directly responsible for making some ministries thrive.

Q6 Do you believe tithing is still relevant?

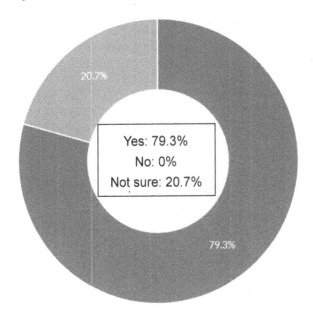

Yes: 79.3%
No: 0%
Not sure: 20.7%

Q7 Based on your experience, how would you suggest godly wisdom should be applied when practising financial generosity?

Answers:

He loves a cheerful giver. Don't give more than you have to cover bills, etc.

I believe 10 per cent tithe is the minimum and then a case of listening to God for other prompts of giving.

I don't believe in giving and then believing that God will provide for you, ie being in debt and tithing, and I think encouraging that is not a positive thing as it can lead to financial abuse and versions of the prosperity gospel. Those two points can be held separately – we all have resources given to us by God and are told to steward them well. We are also told to have faith in God and not worry about the future but depend on Him. We can all give out of whatever little we have, but in proportion.

It is the attitude of our hearts that is most important. Obedience gets us into the zone, but it is our heart motivation that should determine how much we give.

We do need to be wise – God is not asking everyone to give everything away (only one man in the Bible); however, faith should be applied to giving as well so that we don't just stay within a limit.

Generosity is a journey – a faith journey, and so like faith in any area we get stronger in it by using it. For most people that is going to be starting small and building up. The elements of tithing that are key are intentionality/ proportionality/regularity – I think if you can get these started, even by giving £1 a month, then you start to break the fear-hold that finances can have on you and start the journey. Not the place to end but a great place to start.

Giving should be an extension of a personal walk with God through prayer and seeking to discern His will.

When advising people, I always advise to ensure that 'basic commitments' are covered; after that there is scope. Generosity does sometimes mean sacrificial, giving when sometimes you feel you can't.

I believe godly wisdom reminds us that everything we have, we have been given by God; therefore, we give our best, out of our 'first fruits', not just the leftovers. I personally believe God often rewards generosity, although this is not transactional (we don't give to get).

Giving is an act of faith.

You need to be generous financially but you should not let yourself get into debt by giving.

Give out of what you have, not what you don't have, putting the needs of others first.

You manage your own finances as well as your giving. No need to go into debt or be short of money for bills or food.

Don't give out of debt – start small. Build your faith. Try to make it regular – even if it's a £1 a month. Set up a tiny direct debit.

Recognise all your resources are God's anyway. Be consistent in giving.

There's a lot of biblical information about generosity and the whole gospel is founded on the generous loving kindness of the Trinity. Copying Him is the first step, listening to the Holy Spirit to help be effective.

Considering whether giving simply 'maintains' the problem or will bring transformation.

I think it's right for Christians to consider their giving, and ask for God's guidance/wisdom on how to support local ministry and support the causes that are on their heart.

Registered charity donations – a lot of them are very suspect, especially the ones who won't take a donation, but want to sign you up to a plan.

Godly wisdom is necessary when giving money away, as it is not right to waste God's provision in the wrong way. We should first pray into our motive for giving and if it is God's will, we will know a peace about it.

Don't be foolish with the money you have; however, the love of money is the root of all evil.

Knowing that it is a mandate to tithe to God your finances, and by doing so putting your trust in God's wisdom that He knows best for our lives and it builds our relationship and character in Him. Godly wisdom is being able to look past our situations and remain in peace, knowing we are taken care of. But it starts with obedience to His Word. Tithing isn't in the Bible for us to weigh up if it applies to us or not. It was put there to teach us the importance of it, and honouring God's goodness.

In the past, I have personally benefited when I have tithed. When on low income, tithing and stretching my finances by helping others in a financial way has been very rewarding.

With being in debt, we have to make sure that is paid for first; once we pay our creditors, we will tithe from the remaining pay. We understand that being in debt isn't the best place to tithe from, and tithing 10 per cent of our income wouldn't be wise for us. Those without debt should pay a healthy tithe based on gross, or however God is leading them.

Listening to what God tells you and obeying is true wisdom. Stewardship is important but can often be a term used to justify stinginess and a poverty spirit. Likewise, 'logic' can be used to mask fear. Godly wisdom recognises that God has provided all and that if He asks us to give, He will continue to provide for us. He tells us to trust Him with our money, and He will prove His generosity to us.

We are wise stewards of everything that we have been given. I think there is a greater level of accountability now in terms of giving – we want to know where our money is going and does it have impact.

I believe first we need to accept it's not our money but God's. Then ask our Father how He wants us to use it. The Bible tells me our Father wants us to multiply what He's given us rather than hiding it underground and doing nothing.

Godly wisdom is about responding to the prompting of the Holy Spirit; when He prompts, we respond… it may rarely seem like human wisdom, yet the outcome demonstrates far beyond the seen. (Kingdom outcomes.)

Don't give out of debt is an example of wisdom applied to generosity.

Difficult question – wisdom applied in terms of who to give to and in what form? This is challenging as one can fall into being judgemental or cynical. Better to give freely! Wisdom can be used to support organisations that align to our own values and hopes.

Prayer, prayer and prayer! What does God's Word say? When you feel God's prompting, do it even if it makes no sense to you. Remember it all comes from Him anyway. Don't look for man's praise; just be obedient to Him.

Praying about what you have to share and discerning where it should be placed. What are we holding on to that we don't need? How can we be generous in our time and giftings and how can God use that as well?

This is a good question and a big one to answer… I think there are three layers to financial giving. 1. Tithe: your first 10 per cent of income going to the storehouse (the Church). 2. Offerings: this is over and above your tithe and is there

to bless others (organisations, charities and individuals).
3. Generosity: This is extravagant giving of time, talent,
touch and treasure. A lifestyle we live to freely give to
others out of our abundance.

I believe followers of Jesus should tithe first and any
generosity should come from what's left, always giving
with an ear open to hear what the Holy Spirit is saying.

It begins with the tithe. Every Christian is called to tithe.
That's the start of it. My observation would be that those
Christians who tithe are more likely to give to other causes.
The opposite is also true for those who do not tithe. It's not
all about a 'feeling' of the Spirit leading us; sometimes
biblical principles are where Christians need to begin being
generous.

Giving out of the abundance of your heart. Give as you feel
led by the Holy Spirit and not because you feel pressured to
do so against your will.

I just ask Holy Spirit.

For me it's about being obedient to God in action/deed with
a positive attitude – being aware of the leading of the Holy
Spirit, not just need or man.

Give a tenth of all that you earn and then if you can do
more, be more generous. Be the best steward of what you
have with the needs around you.

If you are married, set a limit of what each spouse can give
without agreement from the other. The Bible says two
witnesses. So on really big gifts, I talk to my financial guy
for input.

Giving that grows from a healthy relationship makes a lot
of sense in most instances. Know who we are supporting by

our giving or having taken time to research why our giving to a particular cause is really important. Also, what we are giving to is important – especially as we are stewards of what we have and what we give!

You can never outgive God. I believe tithing is so important and should not be mistreated.

Be led by the Spirit and He will guide you in where to give generously.

Give as God calls you to give.

Completely up to the individual based on character, need and resources available to them... give what you can!

Yes. 10 per cent is a guide. It does not actually translate to a numerically certain biblical principle not least because the biblical world knew nothing of the welfare state, universal healthcare at the point of need, etc. Yet the regular and committed principle is a good one and so is the idea of giving more the more you earn, which to some degree the 10 per cent offers, but the number itself... for some of us that might reasonably be 0.5 per cent and for others 50 per cent.

Seek to act as Jesus wishes us to do.

I think Christians should allow their head to rule their giving, not their emotions. Be aware of manipulation in the realm of giving; it is worth checking an individual or organisation has good financial systems in place.

Through prayer and good knowledge of what you are giving to.

Not something I have thought about, but I guess there needs to be balance with giving so you don't get yourself in need of help!

Q8 What is your favourite scripture or Bible story regarding financial generosity? Why is this your favourite?

Answers:

The woman who gave the smallest amount.

The building of the tabernacle, and later the temple. All who could give did and it was either exactly the right amount needed or the giving was so generous the instruction was to stop.

'Each of you should give what you have decided in your heart to give, not reluctantly or under compulsion, for God loves a cheerful giver' (2 Corinthians 9:7). I think generosity begins in the heart.

Don't have one.

'The world of the generous gets larger and larger; the world of the stingy gets smaller and smaller. The one who blesses others is abundantly blessed; those who help others are helped.'
(Proverbs 11:24-25, The Message*)*

2 Corinthians 8 – Paul relaying the sacrificial generosity of the Macedonian churches – so inspiring.

Luke 21 – widow's offering – always reminds me that being a generosity champion has nothing to do with the amount you give – God is impressed with percentages, not amounts.

The widow's mite – it doesn't really matter how much we give, though it does matter how we give and what is left afterwards!

2 Corinthians 9:6-15.

Zaccheus pays back what he owes (and more) after an encounter with the King. Money shrinks in its importance when we see God's bigger picture.

'God loves a cheerful giver.' It's my favourite because it shows us that we should not be miserly in our giving.

The widow who gave her only coin because she gave everything she had.

Jesus and the coin found in the fish, giving the tenth to Caesar [sic]. Showing God will provide and that it is important to pay taxes even if we don't want to or feel like it.

The widow's offering.

Ananias and Sapphira is the most memorable …

'It is more blessed to give than … receive' [Acts 20:35] cause it's wonderfully true but counterintuitive in a self-centred world.

Mark 12:41-44; Luke 21:1-4: The wealthy made great show of how much they gave but the widow gave despite the cost to her.

Luke 14:15-24, parable of the great banquet. I'm not claiming it is directly about financial generosity. But it speaks of the inclusive hospitality of God's kingdom, which

I think is a good grounding principle for financial generosity.

The widow's mite. She gave all she had without thought to her own needs.

The woman with the olive oil that never ran out.

The poor woman at the temple. Because despite her circumstances she gave all that she had to God because she trusted Him. Her heart was pleasing to the Lord. She didn't make a show of it, but rather quietly gave her offering to the Lord. And through this, God was pleased with her. Isn't that all we seek from the Lord, His approval?

The old lady giving her last pennies. Her gift was loved by God. Mark 12:42-44.

'When you give to the needy, do not let your left hand know what your right hand is doing' (Matthew 6:3). When we give to people in the offering privately and anonymously, this is what we do; we reach into the wallet and take an amount and don't actually know what we have given. The same with time; when you serve you don't know how long you serve for, what this is going to consist of in terms of energy and so you just give.

The widow's mite. I have lived it out and seen it in action. Giving generously is a state of heart, not a state of wallet.

John 10:10, 'life in all its fullness' (GNT) ... abundance. God has given me life, so I want to give and pass on that life to others.

The parable of the sower is a parable of Jesus found in Matthew 13:1–23, Mark 4:1–20, Luke 8:4–15.

2 Corinthians 8 and 9. The church in Macedonia were living life at the lowest ebb yet pleaded to give to a community suffering in a famine back in Jerusalem.

'Therefore do not worry about tomorrow, for tomorrow will worry about itself. Each day has enough trouble of its own' (Matthew 6:34). We should never hold too tightly to anything that can't be used to shape us or someone else into Christ's image. This is a lesson on true trusting of the Father.

Good Samaritan. Generosity beyond boundaries – meeting the needs or someone even when there are reasons not to help, and covering the cost of restoration.

Luke 21:1-4, the widow's mite. It may not have appeared much to man, but it was the widow's everything. It's not necessarily about what you give but how you give it.

Proverbs 22:6 on the value of time; 1 John 3:17; what are we holding on to?

Proverbs 11:24 (The Message) says, 'The world of the generous gets larger and larger; the world of the stingy gets smaller and smaller.' What's interesting about this verse and many others in the Bible about giving is the motivation isn't about what your generosity can do for someone else; it's about what it does for you. Of course, others will benefit when you are generous, but how good is God that when we're generous our world gets larger and larger? What a beautiful principle of His kingdom.

Matthew 6:24-26. Although not specifically about generosity, if we truly believe that God will provide for our needs, then it is easier to give generously without worrying about the future.

171

The widow's offering (Mark 12:41-44). It teaches us to be generous with the little we have and not wait to have more than enough before showing generosity.

The Good Samaritan. Because we don't understand we're being asked to give to 'anyone in need'. That's the moral of the story.

Malachi 3:10 and Matthew 5:16 ... One is about obedience and one is about our actions prompting people to open up to our generous Father in heaven.

'Who am I, and who are my people, that we should be able to give as generously as this? Everything comes from you, and we have given you only what comes from your hand.' (1 Chronicles 29:14)

John 3:16. God is a giver.

Proverbs 3:5-6.

I love the story of the boy with the loaves and the fish. It shows that it isn't the amount you give; it's your heart attitude. Also with giving little, God can multiply it.

The widow and the pennies.

The widow's two mites! She gave above and beyond her means to help others when she herself was probably the most needy... it comes from a heart and spirit of generosity that some people are blind to and do not understand even when they have much.

Don't think I have one...

Elijah and the widow's cruse of oil in 1 Kings 17. Shows the abundant generosity of God which is our model.

Acts 10:38, Not a monetary verse but it says, 'God anointed Jesus ... and ... he went around doing good'. Money itself is neutral, but can do an enormous amount of good! (NB, I don't believe tithing is mandatory; so many people are struggling with cost of living, etc.)

The widow's mite, as she gave from her heartfelt generosity and love for God.

Give and it will come back to you; 'good measure, pressed down, shaken together and running over' (Luke 6:38). I love the thought of our being pressed down so more can be got in. And then it runs over.

The boy with the five loaves and two fish, because it shows what God can do with a little human willingness.

Q9 In your opinion/experience, do you believe the more you practise generosity, the easier it becomes?

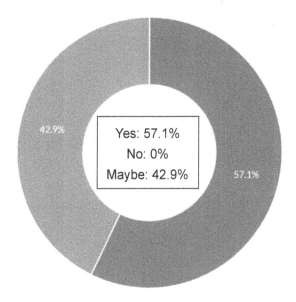

Yes: 57.1%
No: 0%
Maybe: 42.9%

Q10 We know there are *many* amazing stories of generosity shown by individuals, charities and the Church. Can you share your favourite story (this can be your own story)?

Answers:

Received funding as a missionary family to serve in Haiti. Now looking for funding to serve as a Homeland missionary with OMS (One Mission Society).

Cannot think of one at the moment.

It is the approach that a church took when building their church and then the extension. Whatever they received for the building, they gave a percentage (10 or 15, I can't remember) to the poor. The building project was, I believe, £5 million. They were concerned that the building became the priority, which was why they didn't want to neglect their ministry to those in need. Needless to say, they were successful in both areas.

Early days of marriage we wanted to get on the housing ladder but had no deposit. One day I met an old lady in need and gave the money in my pocket, £20, which I really needed. That night a knock on the door and some friends came in and gave us £3K towards a deposit. The next day someone else offered a £3K interest free loan; £6K is what we needed back then and were able to secure a mortgage! God is faithful.

It's God's attention to detail that always gets me more than the amounts. Our daughter's wedding was happening and we were £400 short to make the final payment to the music group doing the reception. We had to pay the band in cash. As the week leading up to the wedding went on, we still didn't have any funds. We didn't tell anyone, just kept praying. On the day before the wedding, I came home at lunchtime and found an envelope through the door – in it was £400… in cash! If it had been a cheque, we couldn't have banked it in time to get the cash out – so God provided in cash.

During a long period of illness and inability to work, we were sustained by the generous giving of many individuals who knew our need and gave freely.

We once had a friend who was in need of finances to return to the UK (stuck abroad). We really wanted to help but were worried about affording our monthly outgoings. Felt God reassure and therefore gave (leaving us short). The next day we received a cheque in the post from a friend wanting to bless us – for more than 3x the amount we had given!

When the church has had a special offering to support a family in financial hardship.

I've bought school uniforms for children who had to move school because of bullying.

I have heard many, many remarkable stories but the most amazing thing to me is that any church of any size is able to function and thrive on the pure generosity and faith of its attendees.

We have been in non-salaried ministry for pretty much our whole working lives. We are living testimony to the provision of God.

Passing on a car to someone who needed it when the previous owner no longer needed it. Has happened quite a lot in our church and we've had/done both.

A friend in church found out we were going to be excluded from a social trip to the zoo. At that time we just couldn't afford it. They bought us an annual membership in order to include us. It actually made me feel a bit uncomfortable. I had to do some processing and consideration of what it meant to be a willing recipient of that gift. I was thankful for it and put aside feelings of pride or that I somehow should be paying for this. It was an open-hearted and natural response from someone who is generous in all things. Though I do think we all need to be careful of the power dynamic of wealth and conscious of how it feels to be a recipient. Sensitivity may be required.

I asked a senior pastor I was under if I could have a raise and he told me the church didn't have the money for it. A while later, he and his wife gave me a gift of £500 from their own finances. I have had so many spontaneous, unsolicited financial gifts from Christians over the years I could barely count.

I have been the recipient of others' generosity over the years both practically and financially. Many years ago, when the Poll Tax was in force, I didn't have enough money to pay it one month. I hadn't mentioned this to anyone but an envelope was popped through my door with the exact amount in cash inside. I have never been good at accepting help but have gradually realised that the blessing goes two ways. I find it easier to give than to receive but by receiving graciously and gratefully, the donor is also blessed.

As a child, the church sourced a house for my family to live in. This may not have been the best solution, some may argue, but as a child scared of sleeping at night because we didn't have our own home that felt safe – knowing the church went out of their way to give us that security showed me more love than I had ever felt or received at that time. Knowing a group of people have your back when you're too tired or weak to stand up for yourself or fight shows more love than anything else. Words can be flippant and meaningless sometimes, but action requires more sacrifice and leaves a lasting impression.

Surprising people by not accepting payment for the parts to repair white goods. The look of gratitude on their faces. Beautiful.

Where do I start? Praying for a car, received one. Praying for petrol when on red, fuel needle raised. Praying for debt clearance, money in offering. Praying for food for child, received that evening. Praying for help with food for household, food bank opened. Praying for a job, job provided with extra income. Praying for a wedding costing less than £1,000, church came together and supplied food, band and DJ! Prayed for a home, someone in the church helped towards our legal fees. Praying for help with my prescription, someone paid a yearly subscription for me! Needed things for our baby, God came through. God seems to give at the eleventh hour all of my Christian life!

When I was a new believer, I was eighteen and had my bank card 'stolen' by the cash machine and returned to my home bank 100 miles away. I had 9p left in my purse and no food in the flat. I was on the way to church and a bit hungry… 9p wouldn't even buy a packet of polo mints so I put it into the collection with no real sense of holiness, more a sense of, 'It's no use to me anyway,' and remembering the widow's mite story. After church I was invited to an old lady's house for lunch and stayed there until the evening service. When I returned home after the evening service, I entered my locked flat and my locked bedroom to find a brown envelope in the centre of my bedroom floor, far from the door. It contained a crisp new £10 note. My flatmates were all away. No one else had keys and no one had entered the flat while I was out. Everything else was exactly where I had left it. I didn't want to use the £10, I wanted to frame my miracle money. But instead I used to it to buy food, which lasted until my card was returned from my home bank branch. Feel free to use this story. 1988, Edinburgh.

An elderly lady gives to us as a youth charity. She sends a cheque each month with her wobbly writing. She never misses a date; she never misses an opportunity. She doesn't want a thank you – she just trusts us. She doesn't want a newsletter; she knows we are making a difference. Every month it reminds me of the story of the widow's mite.

I know many charities that do amazing work. I couldn't pick one because during the lockdown period, I saw so many churches practise such amazing generosity, putting faith back into humanity.

Gift-wrapping to the communities … prior to Christmas. Some astonishing opportunities to explain the gospel and showing generosity and kindness without limit.

I chose to live by faith in my first ministry post. Prayed and sought God for provision and individuals started to bless us. I chose to tithe 10 per cent on everything – even a £10 gift. The generosity then came to me even more so. I was blessed with the rent on a flat, got given two cars and even had a gift of £1,000. We tithed on every monetary gift we received, which led us to believe God could provide anything. A few years later, we were blessed with the full deposit on a house (even after tithing on the gift), and were given a 300-seater chapel for our church (debt free and at no cost). Lots of little stories in one principle that we still live by today.

I'm most moved when I see people be generous out of their poverty. Recently a single mum on benefits, with two young kids, was one of the few who came forward to sponsor a Compassion child.

Every year our church offers free Christmas gift wrapping to the people Christmas shopping in the city. We buy good quality wrapping paper, ribbons, bows and tags. We wrap as many presents as the people need all free of charge, not even taking donations. If people insist on giving money, we ask them to donate to a charity of their choice. Once people get their head around the fact that it's all free it can lead to some great conversations! On one occasion a man insisted we take a £10 donation for our generosity. Within minutes some grandparents asked us to wrap some gifts for their grandchildren. A conversation was had and it turned out that the grandchildren's home had burned down, resulting in the family losing everything. The £10 donation was immediately given to the grandparents so they could buy something extra for the grandchildren. A little later the grandparents returned again with some books they had bought for the grandchildren. They asked that before they were wrapped someone would write on the inside cover, 'With love from the Elim church.' I don't know who was more blessed that day, the original recipient who made the donation, the grandparents, the grandchildren or the Elim church! I think it was everyone!

In 2018, as a church we spoke on financial generosity and wanted to teach the church practically on this. We announced an offering and that we would give the entirety of it away. We raised nearly 40K and were able to bless three local charities in the town. We also did something similar in another church ... and we blessed our town through gifts. Some of the most beautiful stories of generosity though are the private ones – the simple text message that asks someone how they are and to let them know they are thinking of them. This act of generosity is so powerful and often underrated in a possession-driven world.

A few years ago, we were moving home and our church had their annual 'heart for the house' offering. We believe God led us to a financial giving figure – it was way more than we were comfortable giving, but we trusted in faith that God was leading us. Within three weeks every penny came back in and we were able to give to the offering. God is faithful to those who trust Him.

My favourite story is of Dr Richmond Wandera, a former Compassion sponsored child. But through the generosity of his sponsor, he was able to get holistic support. Today, he pastors a church in Uganda, he is the founder and president of Pastors Discipleship Network (PDN). He also sits on Compassion UK's board of trustees.

I've felt led to give a big chunk of my 'pension' away in obedience to Holy Spirit. Didn't see that one coming!

Having tithed and given while our income was nothing but we could financially afford to. Years later we were stepping out in faith with nothing and we never went into the red. As I reflect, I felt God say because [we] sowed then we reaped ... but then I felt God say, 'Never doubt my generosity – my generosity is not based on you but me... but obedience opens the door.'

When I worked for a Christian youth charity, I had a team of supporters who funded at least 50 per cent of my salary – sometimes up to 80 per cent. It was amazing.

I preached about sowing 1 per cent of an idea that God gave you that you can't afford. A man in our church sowed his 1 per cent and had a 100 per cent plus harvest. His thank you to our church was to pay off our mortgage of $1.3 million. Plus, he gave me $100,000 as a thank you for inspiring him.

I think the theme of generosity has sadly become synonymous with money and not with our values. I have discovered that my heart is the greatest barrier or door in my desire to be generous. I have discovered that people can give me their money, but that does not mean that I have their support or heart for the mission God has entrusted to me or the ministry I am leading. Conversely, when I have given finance or anything else, I have discovered that it is because I have already given my heart. Generosity rises from the heart, before it touches other areas that need to be accessed. We share, give and care from the heart, long before we do so from our other resources.

We support a young boy in Kenya and through our giving we are able to put him through his education and he is going to college. When I visited him in the children's home in Kenya I had the immense joy to baptise him in a local river.

Christ who gave His life for us! The ability through Compassion UK to impact and change the lives of many young people in Kenya.

When we worked in London we knew an elderly lady … who had a dreadful life story, having been sold into sex slavery as a child by her father to fund his gambling debts. Somehow, she had survived and lived on a basic state pension in a miserable little … flat. Yet she had a jar on the mantelpiece where she put any loose change she had. She used it to buy cake ingredients. When anyone in our community was having a tough time, she would appear on the doorstep with a cake just to tell us we were loved and that she was praying for us. She had nothing, really, but from what she had she gave something that impacted a whole community.

Church exchange visit to Sri Lanka when a fairly poor man – a bus driver who was a Christian – insisted on lending his mobile phone for over a week while I was staying there so that I could phone home because I couldn't get a signal on mine.

I love the 'little' stories of ordinary people who have given a 'faith gift' out of their need, and God has blessed them with a surprising tax rebate, wage rise or personal gift.

Supporting a woman with two children who had escaped an abusive and violent relationship. The church and individuals helped to rehouse her and provide carpet, furniture and white goods. Repeating the process when she was rehoused again because another resident set fire to the block of flats that she lived in.

I love how one ministry had very little money so they couldn't pay staff. So they gave away what they had and then a miraculous amount of money came in.

The opening story by Robert Morris in his book The Blessed Life *– my favourite ever testimony!*

Appendix 2
Resources for the Journey

To continue growing in the area of financial generosity and therefore becoming more like Jesus, these organisations are a fantastic place to start:

Gospel Patrons is passionate about helping you find and fulfil your part in God's kingdom.
www.gospelpatrons.org

Generous Giving believes biblical generosity changes everything.
www.generousgiving.org

Gospel Entrepreneurs develops people who are inspired, energised and equipped to take a strong Christian lead in church, ministry and business.
www.gospelentrepreneurs.org

Christian Stewardship Network helps to transform your church through financial discipleship.
www.christianstewardshipnetwork.com

Faith Driven Investor is a movement dedicated to helping Christ-following investors believe that God owns it all and that He cares deeply about the how, where, and why behind our investment strategies.

www.faithdriveninvestor.org

The Generosity Report, released on 20th June 2024, gives a greater understanding of the UK Christian giving landscape. This report explores how much Christians are giving, what they think about generosity and why they do or don't give.

www.stewardship.org.uk/generosity-report

Appendix 3
The Thirty-day Generosity Challenge!

This is an exciting and fun challenge that is best enjoyed with the support of others. If you have read this book as a small group, take on the challenge together. If you are doing the challenge alone, ask someone to be your accountability partner with the expectation that you can share your adventures with them. Make use of the list below to record your acts of generosity. As I don't want you to end up bankrupt by the end of the challenge, include a mix of generous acts across the range of time, talent and treasure. I can guarantee it'll be interesting and encouraging to look back on what you have achieved.

If you miss a day, be kind to yourself and do a generous act the following day. Be bold, be creative and look for opportunities to bless others using your time, talent and treasure.

The Thirty-day Generosity Challenge

Day 1:

....
....

Day 2:

....
....

Day 3:

....
....

Day 4:

....
....

Day 5:

....
....

Day 6:

....
....

Day 7:

....
....

Day 8:

....

....

Day 9:

....

....

Day 10:

....

....

Day 11:

....

....

Day 12:

....

....

Day 13:

....

....

Day 14:

....

....

Day 15:

....

....

Day 16:

....

....

Day 17:

....

....

Day 18:

....

....

Day 19:

....

....

Day 20:

....

....

Day 21:

....

....

Day 22:

....

....

Day 23:

....

....

Day 24:

....
....

Day 25:

....
....

Day 26:

....
....

Day 27:

....
....

Day 28:

....
....

Day 29:

....
....

Day 30:

....
....

Now you have completed the challenge, take some time to reflect:

- Consider how many of the acts of generosity you completed were time, talent or treasure, and if one came more naturally. Mark down any particular highlights and ask yourself why this act is a highlight; is it because of how it made you feel, the reaction of the recipient, or something else?

- Spend some time giving thanks to God for His amazing provision that has allowed you to follow in His footsteps, consistently and generously giving to others and blessing them.

- Decide how this will impact your behaviour and thought processes moving forward. How will you continue to follow the example of our abundantly generous God and look for ways to generously bless others?

Please email me at wendy_pawsey@yahoo.co.uk about your stories, adventures and experiences during this challenge. I look forward to hearing from you!